THE POWER OF
DISCERNMENT

THE POWER OF DISCERNMENT

HELPING YOUR TEEN HEAR GOD'S VOICE WITHIN

Maggie Pike

Saint Mary's Press • Winona, Minnesota

Genuine recycled paper with 10% post-consumer waste. Printed with soy-based ink. 50407

The publishing team included Leif Kehrwald, development editor; Mary Duerson, copy editor; James H. Gurley, production editor; Sue Knopf, typesetter; Cären Yang, art director and designer; Paul Krause, cover designer; manufacturing coordinated by the production services department of Saint Mary's Press.

Printed in the United States of America

Printing: 9 8 7 6 5 4 3 2 1
Year: 2011 10 09 08 07 06 05 04 03
ISBN 088489-687-0

Library of Congress Cataloging-in-Publication Data

Pike, Maggie.
 The power of discernment : helping your teen hear God's voice within /
by Maggie Pike.
     p. cm.
 ISBN 0-88489-687-0 (pbk.)
 1. Discernment of spirits. 2. Christian life. 3. Spiritual
life–Christianity. 4. Conduct of life. I. Title.
 BV5083.P55 2003
 248.8'45–dc21

2003002132

I lovingly dedicate this book

to
Eleanor Sheehan, CSJ,
who taught me to discern,

and
Kathy Root,
who discerns with me

I wish to acknowledge the following for their input and support:

Heidi Briscoe; Dolores Curran; Kathy Coffey; Denise Erbele; Mary Ann Figlino, CSJ; Gianeen Hill; Kathy Huling; Dana Radetsky; Mary L. Stokes, BVM; Sue Young; Marylin Withers; the parishioners of Saint Frances Cabrini Church, Littleton, Colorado; those dear spiritual friends who have given me the honor of journeying with them; and Tim, Anne, Betsy, Andrew, and Molly Pike. You have stood in your truth. I'm proud of you.

CONTENTS

INTRODUCTION

DISCERNMENT. That should be easy enough to explain. We use it all the time: I *discern* a tad of sarcasm in your voice. She's very *discerning* when it comes to people's characters. He was horrified when he *discerned* the taste of chili powder instead of cinnamon in a cookie from the same batch he had taken to welcome the new neighbors. All we have to do is flip to the *D*'s in that fat dictionary on the shelf to find a tidy definition of discernment, with references to perceiving, observing, noticing differences, and utilizing keen understanding and insight.

But *discernment* can be a churchy word, too. "Discernment of spirits"—these words fly throughout religious establishments with the grace of a dove. We discern God's will. We discern good from evil. We discern what is of God and what is not. Now the word *discernment* takes on a whole new dimension, a spiritual one. We observe, notice differences, and develop keen understanding and insight to perceive the difference between choices that fill us with life and those that drain life from us, so that we can live healthy lives in harmony with God's vision for us. The simple, three-line dictionary definition of discernment, now infused with faith, takes on deeper meaning. And because it involves human nature interacting with the quiet voice of the Holy Spirit, it also becomes more complex.

This is a book meant to encourage parents to empower their preteens and teens to discern the presence and action of God in their lives. Yet when I was a teenager I had never heard that expression, discernment. In fact, it wasn't until I was in the throes of raising children that I first became aware of what, for me, was a thrilling concept: that God communicates divine will directly to me. Discernment is the gift of the Holy Spirit that I use to listen to God's voice. Teenagers don't have to wait as long as I did. They have the gift, too.

Our Church has always taught that our individual, well-formed conscience is at the heart of moral decisions. This is only possible because of the indwelling Holy Spirit, whose gift to us is discernment, the ability to hear with clarity God's direction for our lives. Our faith informs us that God's revelation is ongoing and that God communicates with us from within. Therefore, we have the ability to hear God if we but listen.

It gets even more exciting. The good news is that God is not inviting us to a dirge, a standing order of suffering and sacrifice, a castor oil spiritual life. Instead, God is drawing us forth into fullness of life, one marked by peace, love, joy—and freedom. To help us along, God has given us the Holy Spirit, complete with the gift of discernment.

What I'm eager to share is that understanding this spiritual gift can be a tremendous support to us in our parental responsibilities. What I can't wait for teenagers to discover is that God really does want us to have freedom—what Bernard Häring calls "the greatest risk God ever took." This is not the anything-goes, let-anarchy-reign, no-boundaries kind of freedom that is, in fact, an abuse of God's gift to us. Instead, God's freedom is spiritual and emotional liberation from those attitudes, habits, and fears that confine us, bind us, and block us from fullness of life. Whether we can accept this gift of freedom hinges on learning to listen to that loving, encouraging, wise voice within.

One of the strongest insults believers can receive—at least, it seems, in the eyes of the one serving it up—is, "They're nothing but cafeteria Christians," meaning they pick and choose only what they want to believe. Such a slanted oversimplification of the intricate and sacred process of listening to God's voice! In my thirteen years of practicing spiritual direction and giving retreats, eleven years of teaching intermediate and high school students, and twenty-five years of raising five children, I've seen that life is laden with choices. The spiritual journey is abundant with choices, and God calls us to make decisions that are moral, loving, and life-giving. The menu is varied—at times unappetizing, at times enticing—but God is the bread of life, and that above all is our staple as followers of Jesus. Indeed, God has given us a divine utensil for making those healthy decisions: the Holy Spirit's gift of discernment. Our role as parents is to teach our children to use discernment, to make decisions that nourish their bodies, minds, and souls.

This theme of teaching families to discern burns in my heart because of the hunger I've seen in people I've known in spiritual direction and on retreats who so genuinely seek God's will in their lives but who are bound by "shoulds" and external expectations. The transformation in these people when they realize that we are truly free beings, centered in a God who loves us unconditionally, who wants nothing more than our greatest good, our utmost happiness, is a miracle indeed. And one I must share.

While *cafeteria Christian* is a pejorative term, indicating someone has an anything-goes attitude about moral decisions, *discerning Christian* has a more authentic ring to it—authentic to our call to live in union with God. Jesus, through whom we come to know God, tells us, "I came so that they might have life and have it more abundantly" (John 10:10). This invitation to fullness of life is precisely the fruit of a spiritual life rooted in discernment. Discerning believers expect God's direction in their lives, listen for it, and follow it to the best of their understanding. They are aware that God dwells within and that, therefore, in addition to the Scriptures, the wisdom of their Church, and the experience of those who have come before, their own experience is the warm water in which the yeast of God's will can grow. Discerning believers have found a better path to knowing God's will than the prepackaged, one-for-all regimes that have previously left them hungry for an experience that confirms God's hand in their decisions. They have, in short, chosen freedom in God.

Discernment is not some kind of glib relativism. Rather, it is a spiritually sound, Scripture-based, tried-and-tested-for-centuries recipe for living in God's will. Discernment of spirits is one manifestation of the Spirit, and is ours to be used for the common good, the building of God's Kingdom (1 Cor. 12:7–11).

Saint Paul advised the Ephesians, and continues to advise us, "Living the truth in love, we should grow in every way into him who is the head, Christ" (Eph. 4:15). What a powerful message to instill in our youth. Growing into Christ is the path to spiritual maturity. It involves finding our truth, that is, seeking what is true and right for us as that truth proceeds from Christ's life in us. It is above all a process. Discernment, too, is a growing process, one that lasts a lifetime. We are all on this journey—children as well as parents.

As I've listened to the stories of people I see for spiritual direction, particularly their sacred realizations of God's presence and action in their lives, I've wondered why we can't begin at an early age teaching children to discern. I recently gave a retreat for a group of young adults, all giving a year of service to poor people. As I spoke with many individually, the same theme kept surfacing. "Tell me more about discernment," they begged. "How can I know I'm doing the right thing?" These were sincere followers of Jesus, trying to make sense of their deep inner longings, trying to reconcile them with the expectations of society, family, their peers, their Church. And with what they perceived God expected of them. The question resurfaced within me: Could we begin even earlier to start talking about discernment in families? Might it actually be possible to make such a lofty-sounding principle as discernment understandable—indeed, practicable—to a ten-year-old, a fifteen-year-old, a young person on the brink of adulthood? Everything in me said yes.

My high school classroom is full of young people who would benefit from being guided in their use of discernment. I often wonder why some resist, rebel, and refuse or bend and buckle, while others unfold so gracefully into the fullness of who they can be.

What is going on in the minds of teenagers who completely disengage from the learning process, refusing to do any assignments? who consistently make unwise choices about companions and activities? who don't seem to like themselves?

What if these same young folks were on top of the world because they knew they were wise, valued, and supported unconditionally? I envision generations of young people who have this kind of emotional, moral, and spiritual confidence because families have made a commitment not to keep them in line but to help them unfold, like gardeners of rare, precious flowers. These families know the gifts of the Holy Spirit, which are ours because God's Spirit abides within us. Parents choose not only to develop these gifts within themselves but also to guide their children in doing the same. In this way, family life is transformed, and souls are transformed.

The wisdom in this book comes from many sources. As much as I would like to, I can't say that I'm writing this book as the result of having systematically introduced the concept of discernment to my children, then successfully led them through the process. On the contrary, I had never even heard of discernment until I was the mother of four, and it took me several years under the guidance of my spiritual director to make discernment a way of life. So a good deal of my insight has come from my own shortcomings in parenting. Indeed, nearly all of the parents I interviewed for this book claim they've spent the better part of their parenting career figuring out the role they play in helping children make mature decisions. They stumble often, fall sometimes, pick up the pieces, and try again—learning volumes in the process. What makes these parents stand out is their sincere desire to raise their children rooted in God's will. Their gracious generosity in sharing their learned wisdom is the heart of this book.

We parents have a challenge in using the gifts God has given us to raise spiritually healthy families. It's scary. Many of us were raised in varying degrees of authoritarian families, where we were told what to do every step of the way, and this has seemed the tried-and-true way to parent. Others of us so desire order in our lives that we see the best way to establish order is to be emphatic about how we want things done in our families. Still others of us know up close exactly what can go wrong in life, and we want to protect our children from any such harm. Something as spiritual as discernment hardly seems tangible enough to raise children with. Letting go and really believing and trusting that God will parent with us is a risk indeed.

So we're embarking on an adventure creating healthy lives from healthy choices. Using discernment to raise children and teaching young people to discern God's truth may be uncharted waters for many, if not most, of us. But it's a method of parenting that is centered in God. It's our best shot.

We can be assured we'll not drown, even when the waters rage. God, after all, is with us through it all.

Chapter 1

BECOMING A DISCERNING ADULT

IT WAS DURING a thirty-week directed retreat—an extended seven-month commitment to daily prayer and weekly guidance of a spiritual director—that I first heard the concept that God could communicate directly to me. I was thirty-six, and it knocked my socks off. Many adults, I've found, are as clueless as I was about listening to the stirrings of God's Spirit within us. I was blessed. I spent eight months meeting weekly with a spiritual director who mentored me in the process of discernment.

The first time I met with her changed me forever. What had prompted my initial visit was a nebulous feeling of inner disorder, which I figured must be spiritual. My director and I talked about my religious history, about who God was for me, about the Holy Spirit's gifts of peace, love, and joy that filled me—or didn't. Soon I found myself talking about a predicament that was causing me deep turmoil within. I was afraid it wasn't spiritual enough to talk about in this setting, but my gentle guide wisely encouraged me to continue.

Here is the story: I had made friends with a single mother of four young boys. I particularly enjoyed this woman's friendship because we connected in a spiritual way. From time to time, she would ask me to care for her children while she met appointments, which I was glad to do. But as time went on, I realized that her "appointments" were actually activities that conflicted directly with my values. She knew this, of course; hence, the deceit.

As I look back on this relationship, I see it with different eyes. But at the time, I believed that helping this woman was charity. I thought it was virtuous to be there for her even as she acted from a different, seemingly misguided, value system. As a sincere follower of Christ, I was certain that God was calling me to put my own needs and desires aside and give, then give some more. I was sure I was doing the right thing, even though it felt horrible.

My spiritual director saw something quite different. I expected her to affirm what I was doing and to give me a theological verification along the lines of how good it must be because I was feeling so bad. Instead, after hearing me describe my inner turbulence, my confusion, disorder, and chaos, she asked, "Do you *want* to be her friend?" I answered that I felt I *needed* to be her friend.

She repeated the question: "But do you *want* to be friends with this woman who has used you, lied to you, and disregarded your values?"

When she put it that way, it was easier to answer.

"No!" I shouted.

"Then that's your answer," she replied quietly.

My spiritual director, in her wisdom, could see that I was extending myself from an unhealed place and that I was ignoring my intuition, my own inner wisdom, which was speaking to me loud and clear through my feelings of distaste for the situation. She initiated me into the practice of discernment, which, much to my surprise, was not something "out there" but was, rather, as grounded in real life as well-worn sneakers, frayed laces and all.

The fruits of discernment, begun that day, were far-reaching. Because I was now able to discern, I could pass on this sacred legacy to my children. And I could do so with great excitement and conviction.

WHAT IS DISCERNMENT?

I have a sneaking suspicion that most of us have already had numerous experiences of discernment, but have never given it a name. Let's think back to the plethora of decisions we've already made in life: The house search that culminated in the day we walked into what we knew with certitude was "our" house. The job interview that triggered repulsion, causing us to turn on our heels practically before the interview was over. The times we knew exactly when to say no and when to say yes to all those requests for our time. Why we told one child no and another child yes. The book we couldn't get into years ago, but now speaks to us on a deep level.

Discernment is a gift of the Holy Spirit through which we come to know God's will for us. We can also think of God's "will" in different terms: God's desire for us. God's hope for us. The dream God shares with us. Wisdom is the foundation of discernment, which is based on our faith that God is continuously communicating with us. God can choose to convey divine insight through a number of instruments: the Scriptures, the wisdom of the Church, spiritual reading, spiritual directors, music, nature, spouses, friends, children, parents. When I gave directed retreats, people often asked how I chose the Scripture passages I assigned them. They were amazed at how specifically God spoke to them in that particular text. I smiled to myself, knowing that I could have thrown in an article from the *Rocky Mountain News,* and the Spirit still would have spoken. That's how powerful and how personal the Holy Spirit is.

God's Spirit works through varied avenues, but many people are surprised to hear that God also communicates *directly to our souls.* For some, God's communication might come as spiritual insights, almost like spoken words. For others, it can come in the form of deep and persistent longing, emotions, preferences, gut feelings, visions, and dreams. Nevertheless, not all internal movement springs from the life-giving source of the Holy Spirit. Saint Paul lists the gifts from God for the building of the Kingdom (1 Cor. 12:4–11). The gift of discernment of spirits is our ability to distinguish God's stirrings from those that rise out of our broken selves, our immaturity, or from evil sources. God's direction is designed to bring us to fullness of life (John 10:10). It is always for our greater good. Attention to this quiet voice within—the subtle, gentle nudges of the Spirit toward goodness, light, and life—is the task of discernment.

INTUITION

Clearly, intuition plays a large role in discernment. How countercultural! I remember the first time I took the Myers-Briggs Type Indicator. This is a personality inventory that has been used widely for understanding personality differences. The results showed that I was intuitive and feeling, but that I was weak in the realm of thinking. My heart sank. I felt like I had received the ultimate insult. But I've come to appreciate my intuition as a gift from God. We use it *in tandem with* reason to discern God's will. But we never ignore it *in favor of* reason.

For example, imagine being in a situation like Gwyneth Paltrow's character in the movie *Sliding Doors.* She decided to board the subway, which led to a particular story line, and—like a logically illogical dream—she also decided *not* to board the subway, which resulted in

her life playing out quite differently. Suppose a man—
we'll call him Sam—hops onto the subway and miraculously meets the perfect woman. Over the next year, he
discovers they share the same faith, values, goals, interests, and talents. His checklist is complete. They become
engaged. This must be the right woman for him, he reasons, because she has all the qualities he wants in a life
partner. As the engagement progresses, however, he has
misgivings. Something is not right, but he can't put his
finger on it. In fact, he asks to postpone the wedding,
which brings his fiancée to tears. After a few months, she
asks him to make a decision and set a firm date for the
wedding. Sam decides that because he can't think of any
reason not to marry this wonderful woman, he'll put
aside his seemingly irrational doubt and commit to her.
He has ignored his intuition in favor of reason.

Now roll the cameras back a step or two. Sam gets
pushed out of the overcrowded subway and has to wait
for the next one. Once aboard, he miraculously meets
the perfect woman. Over the next year, he discovers they
share the same faith, values, goals, interests, and talents.
His checklist is complete. They become engaged. This
must be the right woman for him, he reasons, because
she has all the qualities he wants in a life partner. Not
only that, but his whole being is devoted to her, body,
mind, and spirit. As the engagement progresses, his love
deepens, and he becomes more and more certain that
marriage is the right decision. Sam is using intuition *in
tandem with* reason to discern God's will in his choice.

I use the example of marriage choice to illuminate
how to integrate intuition and reason because most of
our young adults will face this choice someday. One

loving, spiritual mother gave this well-intentioned but misguided advice to her distressed daughter, Debbie: "Honey, I know you're having doubts, but think of it this way. If God didn't want you two to meet, he wouldn't have put Jerome in your path. Thank God for him and move forward." She did as her mother suggested, but Debbie's intuition had been right. The marriage lasted only two years.

The shift from our society's overemphasis on reason, then, may be in learning to trust that our intuitive experiences are rooted in God and that they are a valid means of leading us to truth. The Scriptures verify that God sent the Holy Spirit to guide us on our path to union with God.

John 14:16–17. Jesus promises to send the Advocate, the Spirit of Truth, whom we will recognize because the Spirit is within us.

John 14:26. Jesus assures us that God will send the Holy Spirit in Jesus' name and that this Spirit will instruct us in everything.

1 Cor. 2:4–5. Saint Paul tells the Corinthians that his message and preaching don't have the persuasive force of so-called wise argumentation, but the convincing power of the Spirit. As a result, our faith rests on God's power rather than on human wisdom.

1 Cor. 2:6–11. Saint Paul informs us that the spiritually mature know the wisdom that God has revealed through the Spirit. He affirms, further, that no one knows his or her innermost self better than the person's own spirit within.

Matt. 10:19–20. Jesus reassures his Apostles, and us, not to worry about what we'll say or how we'll say it. When the time comes, the Holy Spirit will give us what we are to say.

Rom. 8:26–27. Saint Paul assures us that when we don't know how to pray or what to pray for, the Spirit will pray in us.

Acts 17:28. We live, move, and *are* in God.

The evidence is indisputable: God is with us always, dwelling within, revealing divine wisdom unceasingly.

LONGINGS

In addition to trusting the role of intuition in discerning God's voice, we also want to trust our deepest yearnings, recognize internal clarity, and heed disquieting voices such as fear, doubt, and the feeling that something is not right. We have the Commandments, a mature, informed understanding of the Scriptures, and the wisdom of the People of God, the Church, to support us in making spiritually mature decisions. But most important is the truth that abides in the silence of our hearts, where God dwells.

Let's take an internal poll. All those who grew up thinking that longings were valid expressions of God's will for us, tap your toes. We should be feeling thunderous vibrations across the earth. But sadly, all is quiet. Our God wants fullness of life for us. Yet many of us are living only half-full lives—by choice. We live under the mistaken impression that God calls us to what we would least like to do.

I remember a conversation with Mary, my best friend in high school. We used to hike to a nearby park for our most philosophical discussions, and it was there, perched on a fallen branch, that Mary poured out her most pressing worry. "I just know God is asking me to become a nun," she moaned. "And that just makes me so sad. I've always wanted to meet a wonderful man, get married, and have children. I don't understand God's ways. But I'm going to do God's will, like it or not." Even then, that didn't sound right to me. The young women I knew who had entered the convent did so by choice, fueled by a longing. Fortunately, Mary, too, followed her dream and raised two beautiful daughters.

What if we were to change our paradigm and *assume* that God is the author of our longings, visions, and dreams? When we establish the intent to discern the interior movement of the Spirit, our yearnings seem to rise to the surface. When we can change our prayer from "What do you want *of* me?" to "What do you want *for* me?" we are open to the gifts God wishes to bestow on us. When we make the shift from trying to manipulate God into giving us what we want, to waiting in grateful expectation of what God has in store for us, we examine all with the mind of Christ (1 Cor. 2:16). We have the foundation for healthy decisions.

Saint Ignatius of Loyola, the founder of the Jesuits, has much to share about discernment, including his Rules for Discernment. Indeed, Ignatius's charism was discernment, as is that of his followers, who acknowledge discernment as the heart of their retreat work and spiritual direction. Joseph A. Tetlow, SJ, in his handbook *Choosing*

Christ in the World (Saint Louis: Institute of Jesuit Sources, 1989), explains the discernment of spirits in this way:

> We need to ask of each significant action and of every deep and persistent desire: . . . Does this desire proceed truly out of Christ's life in us, and does its enactment deepen Christlife? We will find out what God hopes for us and in us not only in the desire, but in the enactment, and in the consequences of the enactment. Discernment requires attention to all these stages. . . .
>
> This is the basic question in discernment of spirits: Does my desiring rise from the Spirit of Christ, or from one of the other dynamics? Am I moved by the Spirit of Christ? Am I moved by the spirit of fallen flesh? Am I moved by the spirit of noble humanity? Am I moved by the spirit of the lie? (P. 246)

CLARITY

In discerning God's sometimes all-too-quiet voice, we look for internal clarity. When we're attempting to discern God's will, it isn't the clear-cut, good-and-evil moral issues that cause us problems. Instead, what can trip us up are those decisions that are neither demanded of us nor forbidden. What will further the Kingdom? What will be more life-giving? What will more authentically reflect God's hope for us to be free, whole, and full of life? What makes discernment so frustrating are those times when several courses of action fulfill the requirements equally.

With experience, we'll learn to look for the choice beneath the choice. When we wish to buy a new house, for example, is our deepest desire the house itself, or are we yearning for change in another, less obvious part of our life? Is it external or interior change we're longing for? If we're basing our decision on the wrong foundation, it will not lead us to a fuller life.

Clarity comes in one of several ways to those who discern. On a lucky day, an insight comes almost immediately. We trust it, act on it, and don't look back. This is nothing short of a gift. For most decisions, however, we enter into a process where we weigh the pros and cons and examine them until one choice or reason rises more decisively than the others. Or we focus on how we're reacting interiorly—what we *feel*—as we reflect on each choice. What we're looking for is a peace that may defy logical explanation. Even if the decision itself was agonizing, we experience an increase and deepening of one of the other fruits of the Holy Spirit: love, joy, patience, kindness, generosity, faithfulness, gentleness, self-control (Gal. 5:22–23). It is helpful to verbalize our discernment with another spiritually mature person who can illuminate what we can't see. Many believers seek a spiritual director for this purpose.

Disquieting voices also are worth listening to. I attended an evening of discernment once, and a woman asked this question of the speaker: "If the elevator door opens and only one other man is in there, and everything in me trembles with fear, should I get in?" The answer from the speaker was an unequivocal no. Trust your instincts. It doesn't matter if the man is perfectly innocent; what matters is how you feel at the moment. Unsettling feelings such as fear, doubt, sadness, and anger can inform us that a decision is not authentic to God's desire for us.

Of course, we want to examine those feelings. If rooted in unhealed issues, they may in fact be barriers to clearly discerning God's path. I once knew a man who changed jobs frequently. He always had a good reason: the people he worked with were intolerable. He was fooling himself into thinking that God was leading him to new opportunities. His pattern of anger around his work situations was a red flag that healing needed to take place before he could authentically hear God's voice.

Disquieting feelings, however, are more likely valid signals to probe more deeply into the direction we're about to choose. A friend told me about an interview she had right out of law school: Anxious to obtain a position and begin her career, she approached the interview with excitement and optimism. Ten minutes into the conversation, however, she was troubled by misgivings. Before much longer she was filled with distaste. "Something came over me, and I did something unlike anything I'd ever done before," she reflected. "I stood up, thanked the man for his time, and told him I didn't see any reason to continue the interview. I wasn't interested in working for him."

PRAYER

Becoming a discerning adult means praying, not only in the uttering of words but more specifically in the attitude of lifting our minds and hearts to God. Even more than an activity, prayerful discernment is a way of life. We ask God's help in deciding well, stating our intent that our choice be a reflection of God's desire for our highest good. As the decision-making process progresses, we continue to turn to God in prayer for affirmation of our choice or continued guidance until we experience a deepening of the fruits of the Holy Spirit around the decision. If we have drifted away from prayer, spiritual directors are willing to explore various forms of prayer with us. Many books on prayer also are available. But the surest path to growing in prayer is to show up each day and speak to our loving God from the heart.

Families can benefit from discovering these guidelines for discernment and implementing them in their lives. Families grow in faith when given opportunities and encouragement to practice discernment in concrete ways. If we are equipped with a thorough understanding of the discernment process, as well as the experience of discerning as a way of life, we can be powerful teachers for our children.

Chapter 2

DISCERNMENT AND DEVELOPING A HEALTHY IMAGE OF GOD

WE CANNOT fully experience the freedom of discernment if we have an image of God as one who judges harshly, punishes, and sees us as innately flawed. Depending on the spiritual climate in which we were raised, we as adults may need to repave this part of the road. Clearly, until we know God as a compassionate, loving, totally accepting God, we cannot pass on this image to our young people.

Dennis Linn, Sheila Febricant Linn, and Matthew Linn have written a superb book entitled *Good Goats: Healing Our Image of God* (New York: Paulist Press, 1994), which pins the tail squarely on the stubborn remnants of erroneous concepts about God that trample our faith. With humor and straightforward wisdom, it broaches subjects such as judgment, punishment, and an intimidating God-character called Good Old Uncle George. The Linns attempt to dispel dangerous myths that have been major roadblocks in helping the faithful to develop a healthy spirituality. Some of the beliefs we hold about God are in fact outrageous distortions, directly contrary to what we see in the Scriptures and do nothing less than instill fear about God. In truth, God is desperately reaching out to us in gentle love, which for many, is an incredible gift and a huge relief.

THE GOD OF LOVE

The Scriptures bear out the loving nature of God. John tells us that God loved us first (1 John 4:19). Think of all the times when we had to be the initiators in a relationship. Hanging over our heads was always the cloud of rejection. I remember a time when my husband and I went to the movies with another couple. Several weeks later I called them to see if they wanted to get together again. Faye didn't even hold her hand over the receiver when she asked her husband: "Hey Curt? Wanna go out with the Pikes? Yeah, me neither." Then to me, "Naw." When we've experienced a few rejections like that, it's hard to believe that God loved us first.

In reality, God's love is more like that of another couple, Jerry and Jen, who invited us over shortly after they met us, saying, "We'd like to get to know you better. We were really caught by you." My heart did flip-flops, so elated was I at the compliment. They had loved us first.

God's love as verbalized through the prophet Isaiah shows us how truly pure God's love is:

> I have called you by name: you are mine. . . .
> . . . You are precious in my eyes . . .
> and . . . I love you.

(Isa. 43:1–4)

The love we've known often attaches a tag to that expression of devotion: I love you *because* . . . , I love you *in spite of* . . . , I love you *so that* . . . , and so on. I call this counterfeit love. I've been told that when people are trained to detect counterfeit money, they don't examine the bogus currency but rather the real thing. They become so familiar with real money that they recognize phony bills instantly. So, too, with love. If we, along with our children, believe that God's love is ours without strings, then we are open to receiving the countless manifestations of God's love—the real thing. As Dewitt Jones, photographer for *National Geographic,* said, "When we believe it, we'll see it."

John says further that God is love (1 John 4:8). We can conjure up all sorts of perceptions of love, depending on the quality of love we've experienced in life, how lovable we perceive ourselves to be, personality factors, or where we are in the cycle of life. In my retreat work, I've heard countless stories of women and men who cannot connect with God as love. More than one person, for example, has moaned, "I can't call God Father [or Mother] because of how my father [or mother] treated me." One woman questioned what love means based on her experience with a religious marriage support group whose members stabbed one another in the back while parroting the words "I love you" at every meeting.

Lack of self-love, too, can impede our acceptance of God as love. Some of us have damaged self-esteem from what Thomas Keating calls "the junk of a lifetime," while others of us feel disgusted with ourselves only once a month. Either way, love of God and love of self are ultimately inseparable, and "God is love" doesn't make sense to someone who doesn't love herself or himself.

The Linns propose a deceptively simple thought: God loves us at least as much as the person who loves us the most does (*Good Goats,* p. 11). Sadly, perhaps the person who loves us the most has actually behaved in a dysfunctional way. Even the best of caretakers and spouses reflect the human condition. But God is not dysfunctional.

So let's daydream a bit and create the ideal person-who-loves-us-the-most, and maybe we'll come close to describing our God of love. When I ask the question, "Who is God for you?" at retreats, I hear (in addition to "I have no clue. I'm still trying to figure it out!") these answers: "God is the only one who loves me unconditionally." "God is my best friend." "God is my source of peace." "God is more patient with me than I am with myself." "God is the one I turn to for compassion when I'm really bummed."

Our teens need to know such a God. Many of us cringe when we hear that children's first impression of God is through the person of their primary caretakers. Images of all the mistakes we made in parenting besiege us like a swarm of hornets. Yet I once heard something about how children turn out well if their parents are good parents 75 percent of the time. Twenty-five percent is a generous leeway for bad-humor days. What is important, I believe, is that we verbalize to our children God's love for them, point it out in every manifestation of goodness and beauty, and be comforted knowing that at least 75 percent of the time, our love is the greatest witness they have to God's love. Then we must forgive ourselves when we aren't stellar parents, knowing that God has many ways to reveal love to our youngsters.

DISMANTLE THE WATCHDOG GOD

Nevertheless, many of us harbor the "just in case " syndrome. We find we're carrying a mild dose of anxiety in our actions and decisions—just in case God really is the crazed henchman we once heard about. I'd better make a larger contribution to my church, volunteer to watch my friend's children, head the church committee—just in case God really does have strict expectations of me.

A woman told me, sheepishly, about a time she had warned her son that God was always watching, so he'd better not even think about sneaking any of the fresh-baked brownies while she was out of the room. An extra set of eyes keeping our kids in line may make our job easier, but when we ascribe those eyes to God, we imprint an image of God in their minds that is simply not accurate. When we attempt to teach them to discern, we then have to dismantle the watchdog God and construct a sense of personal integrity rooted in God, who is love.

Perhaps a better understanding of God's role in our decisions is the image of the endlessly patient parent or spouse who takes glee in the risks we take, stands as a safety net as we venture out, enfolds us in the mesh of compassion if we fall, and bounces us onto our feet to try again. What a far cry from a God who disparages our efforts with the overbearing admonition that failure will be considered a personal insult.

Jesus reveals who God is with these words: "I came so that they might have life and have it more abundantly" (John 10:10). This concept is key when helping kids discern. If we succumb to the notion that God is asking us to seek a life of suffering, sacrifice, and self-denial, imagine the path our decisions will follow. Assuredly, life will present plenty of opportunities to endure pain without our ever having to make a choice. But if the nature of God really is to lead us to fullness of life, then our decisions will have a unique face.

JANELLE AND JORDAN

Imagine this scenario. Thirteen-year-old Jordan and Janelle have been best friends for many years, having grown up in the same neighborhood. Yet they had been raised in very different homes. Jordan's parents had presented God to him primarily through the lens of the One who expects much of us, who asks us foremost to sacrifice, to look with suspicion on our desires. Jordan consequently took on the attitude that whatever decision he made should have a feel of dread about it. If a decision was exciting, it must be the wrong choice.

Janelle's parents, on the other hand, had always told her that God wanted her life to be full and happy and that, although hardship would inevitably come, God did not ask her to make decisions that would knowingly lead her to being miserable. In other words, Janelle knew that God was on her side.

One day toward the end of the school year, Janelle and Jordan were hanging out with friends talking about summer opportunities for community service. The guidance department had given them a list of nonprofit organizations looking for young people to help. Some of the friends were excited about mowing lawns for senior citizens, helping in soup kitchens, and tutoring struggling students in reading and math. Not surprisingly, though, Jordan and Janelle latched onto the same posting: "Students wanted to work at a stable that provides therapeutic riding for children with disabilities." Both kids adored horses, and while they didn't know too much about children with disabilities, they loved playing with young kids. The two best friends went home to share their eagerness with their parents.

Jordan's parents reminded him that he should examine his excitement and make sure that his will was also God's will. In their opinion, mowing lawns for older people was a more valuable task than leading kids around on horses, and because Jordan hated mowing lawns, the sacrifice would please God. Jordan reluctantly agreed with his parents, then shuffled out the door, shoulders slumped, to share his news with Janelle.

Janelle's parents, upon hearing the options for community service and discussing each with their daughter, assured her there were no bad choices, that, in fact, all had value. Then they asked her these questions: What do you want to do? Which work will make you feel more happy and alive? Reminding Janelle that a sign we're using our gifts is that we enjoy what we're doing, they invited her to reflect on which job would best use the gifts God gave her. After Janelle made her decision, her parents asked one last question: How does it feel? They knew to look for the hallmarks of peace, clarity, and assurance. Janelle bounced out of the house, ecstatic over her decision to work at the stable.

GOD TRANSFORMS US

Developing an accurate image of God also includes attention to Paul's explanation that God's Spirit is embodied in words like love, joy, peace, patience, kindness, generosity, and gentleness (Gal. 5:22–23). We have a loving God, a joyful God, a peaceful, patient, kind God, a generous God, a mild God. What an affront to this God to ascribe ogre qualities in lieu of those revealed in the sacred Scriptures!

Young people, in their innocent wisdom, must surely see conflict in an illogical explanation that they should fear the One they love. Such an image cannot possibly promote buy-in to the notion of discernment on the part of our adolescents. Jesus tells us repeatedly that ours is a God who honors the *spirit* of the law—the spirit of love—in contrast to the Pharisees, who insist on the *letter* of the law (Matt. 15:11). We don't want our teens to agonize over their actions and decisions as if God were waiting with a sledgehammer to whack them as they round the corner.

Developing a healthy image of God involves examining our own personal experience of God throughout our lives. If we see God as one who punishes, we might first examine what life experiences cemented this image for us. Often, our image of God is formed by our early impressions of the adults in our lives. Similarly, we become like the God we worship (Linn, *Good Goats,* p. 7). If we know a heartless God, for example, we, too, will judge without compassion. Yet if we know a God of endless mercy and unconditional love, this is the God our children will know because they will know parents who are like this God. Our faith informs us that when we center ourselves in God, God transforms us. This transformation implies healing, including all that has damaged our image of God.

As parents, we can guide our children and teenagers to tune in to their experiences of God. We can share these experiences as a family, thus opening one another's eyes to this everyday miracle. In so doing, our young people are building a history of God's loving presence and action in their lives, a history they can turn to often, especially in times of doubt or hardship.

Chapter 3

QUALITIES OF A CO-DISCERNING PARENT

THE ANNOUNCEMENT in the Sunday bulletin seemed harmless enough: "Coordinator of Adult Education is welcoming parishioners to take part in a one-month directed retreat. Call the church office for information." My young children were successfully keeping me fragmented, so I approached this invitation cautiously. Anything that reeked of accountability, reliability, or deadlines was out of the question. Nevertheless, something was drawing me to make the phone call.

Without having a name for it, I was about to enter spiritual direction, the heart of which is discernment. There I would find not the pressure of performing but unconditional acceptance of who I was and where I was on the spiritual journey. Instead of being "directed" along a certain path by my spiritual companion, I was empowered to listen to God's direction for me, using tools for discernment that have become invaluable gifts.

I have been meeting with my spiritual director for sixteen years, and have responded to the call to become a spiritual director myself. Out of my own transformation through spiritual direction, and from the insights I've gained directing other adults, I share some thoughts on how to help kids discern.

PARENTS HELPING KIDS DISCERN

As co-discerners with their children, parents manifest the qualities of a spiritual director. As spiritual companions to our kids, we continually guide, encourage, and assist them as they seek God's hope for their lives and, in so doing, deepen their union with God. The wisdom and experience of spiritual directors throughout the history of the Church reflect common themes when describing the qualities of such a guide. Two of these qualities, experience and common sense, make it all the more appropriate for parents to assume the role of spiritual guide (Kevin G. Culligan, ed., *Spiritual Direction: Contemporary Readings* [Locust Valley, NY: Living Flame Press, 1983]).

The following qualities are also necessary for successful spiritual guidance:

Fidelity to prayer. Discernment happens in prayer. Spiritual directors pray for those they direct. They also pray constantly for wisdom as they embark on this most sacred calling. In prayer, continuously lifting our minds and hearts to God, we come to discern the divine voice as it speaks to us from within, in the Scriptures, and through others. Prayer yields spiritual fruit—increased faith, hope, and love—which infuses us with peaceful, joyful, patient, kind, good, and generous hearts. These are the principle qualities of an effective spiritual mentor.

Anyone seeking spiritual direction would hope the director is a prayerful person. Kids deserve the same. The fruits of the Holy Spirit manifested in our words, actions, and personality are a dead giveaway that we are prayerful. Modeling a prayer life to kids makes a powerful impression. One of my earliest memories is seeing my parents kneeling at the end of their bed at night praying silently. Young folks who see their parents praying, attending retreats, receiving the Eucharist, taking part in the ministry of the Church, and reading spiritual books receive an unspoken message that God is present and active in their lives.

Humility. From conversations with women and men on retreat, I find that people of faith often misunderstand humility. Somewhere along the line, we have absorbed the idea that to be humble means to be self-effacing, to deny what is good and strong in us for fear of sounding vain or proud. On the contrary, true humility means acknowledging that God has endowed us with gifts, thanking God for those gifts, and using them proudly to build the Kingdom.

As we enter into the role of spiritual companion to our kids, we humbly acknowledge that the Holy Spirit is the real guide. Indeed, God reveals divine self to our kids through any number of channels, and so we take seriously the privilege to be our children's most important influence while they are in our homes.

Humility also recognizes that God's providence leads each young person along a path that is uniquely his or hers. God's providence can be difficult to face when it seemingly conflicts with our specific hopes and plans for our kids. Yet it can also be freeing. We must simply listen to God's direction, along with our kids, then enter into the adventure with excitement and trust. To superimpose our own expectations is to confine God. Humility asks that we honor what is authentic for our children, even if it differs from what we would choose for ourselves.

Trust. Well, now, herein strikes a chord. Many of us were quite free spirits before we had children; then, mysteriously, trepidation set in. Parenthood carries enormous responsibilities, rendering the temptation to stick to the most conservative path imaginable nearly overwhelming. As we make the commitment to trust God, and our kids, we might well have to label ourselves "recovering control freaks," for we will surely be lured back into that straight-jacket on many occasions. Trusting our teens becomes particularly difficult when we recall the poor choices we made as adolescents. Remember, though, that as co-discerning parents, we are not relinquishing responsibility, nor are we letting our kids run wild without supervision. On the contrary, we are right there with them as they make their decisions. We are simply not making their choices for them. We empower, rather than weaken, our children with each decision we entrust to them.

Parents must trust and cooperate with the spiritual journey of transformation. I often hear parents say, "She's a good kid. It's just that . . ." Yes, our children are good. If we see kids as inherently flawed, then we tend to break down those human parts of our kids that are not yet transformed rather than supporting their search for what is good and right. God is transforming! This is the essential vision of spiritual mentoring. I once saw a plaque in a child's room that said: "Be patient with me. God isn't finished with me yet." I would add, "Trust that God is working in me." God is creating God's image and likeness in our children's souls as surely as in ours.

Trust empowers the spiritual director to give her or his directees freedom. In contrast to using an authoritarian approach, a good spiritual director fosters an atmosphere where the directees can freely live out the Gospel as they believe is best for them. Parental co-discernment seeks to help kids discover God's will in their lives. Ultimately, we want them to be able to make sound decisions independently. The more freedom we can entrust to them, the more confident they'll grow in this process, so full of discovery and mystery.

By our trust, we affirm our adolescents' integrity. Co-discerning parents will not ask a child to do something that contradicts his or her well-formed conscience. A woman told me that not one of her three daughters got through middle school without an abhorrence for "eating animals." They each went through a vegetarian phase where eating meat plagued their conscience relentlessly. While she did increase their vitamins, Barb never required the girls to eat meat as long as it was so troublesome to them. In a small way, this affirmed their integrity on an issue that was important to them, paving the way for more serious discernment in coming years.

Acceptance. Without acceptance all relationships are stymied. The person meeting with a spiritual director is likely to close up in the face of judgment, leaving the spiritual director without the necessary information to move forward. Acceptance, respect, patience, and sympathetic understanding are powerful tools for facilitating the interior movement that is a hallmark of discernment. Our young adults are no different. If they feel like they can say just about anything without fear of rejection or judgment, they'll talk.

But acceptance must be sincere and unconditional, never manipulative. One of the early lessons of parenthood is recognizing that each child is unique. As a struggling gardener, I think of kids as flowers in a bouquet, their very differences giving the bouquet its beauty. Each flower has its unique requirements for nurturing—just the right amount of sun and water, and the right soil—in order to bring it to the pinnacle of health and splendor. Growing roses and impatiens under identical conditions has never worked for me, which is why the garden society doesn't sponsor tours at my house.

Children, too, have differences that must be honored. Can they sense our awe simply for who they are? Can they detect our interest and fascination in their uniqueness? Can they see how deeply we've fallen in love with them? Amid this undiminished acceptance, kids will be honest about what brews in the depths of their souls rather than sticking to what they think we want to hear. (Sometimes, a mixed blessing!)

We must make every effort to understand the words behind their words, those longings so deep they can't find a way to express them. As co-discerning parents, we create informal, leisurely, friendly settings that encourage kids to share openly. We listen with interest in our eyes, nodding occasionally to indicate we're following, clarifying to make sure we understand, all the while searching for signs of God's gracious activity in the depths of our teens. We respect the sanctity of their growth, and we honor their freedom to listen and respond to God's hope for them without forcing any particular biased plan or answer.

Chapter 4

TOOLS FOR CO-DISCERNMENT

PRAYER, humility, trust, acceptance. Now our kids have trusted allies. We're off to a good start. But if that isn't enough, I will add three more advantages that co-discerning offers our adolescents: objectivity, self-discovery, and a history of God's guidance.

Directing our young adults in discernment offers them the objectivity that is often lacking when they are too close to the situation. They *need* us to accompany them on this journey, whether they acknowledge it or not. Spiritual mentoring also provides a structure for self-discovery. Because knowledge of self and knowledge of God go hand in hand, a practice of discernment under our guidance brings them closer to God. Finally, the process of discernment helps kids build a history of God's guidance from within, and is something they can return to for future decisions.

With every good choice, our teenagers deepen their freedom. A few tools for co-discernment will support our efforts to empower our youth. Using these instruments will provide them with objectivity, facilitate self-discovery, and impart an awareness of God's interior guidance.

While *some* young people will have *some* direct spiritual experiences where they know with certitude what God's will for them is, most will have the less clear *human* experience of conscious deliberation—weighing the pros and cons and talking the decision through before coming to assurance. This is precisely why we're their mentors. At first we will surely be leading them through the second, more human process in order to empower them to discover the first, the direct communication of God to their souls. Undoubtedly, for the rest of their lives, discernment will be a combination of both experiences.

We might also keep in mind that our youth will arrive at some of their decisions simply because it's the right thing to do. They do their homework, show up at work when they're scheduled, stick around when relatives come to visit, observe chastity, nourish their faith life. Pondering alternatives to the family's values is not an option at this stage of their lives while we're mentoring them. Trying their wings comes soon enough.

HELP KIDS DELINEATE BETWEEN CHOOSING AND THE CHOICE ITSELF

Here, we are challenged to let go of expectations for one particular outcome—admittedly contrary to our nature as parents! For years now, we've been guiding our children under a moral system, so the decisions we're helping them with are likely not a question of right or wrong. Rather, we help them discern which option is more authentic for them. Which choice is more life-giving? Which decision will satisfy a persistent longing? Clearly, this is a process, and the process is essential to the decision.

For example, it's not as important whether Jamie chooses going out for the soccer team over taking a part-time job as it is that her choice evolves from reflection, over time, on her gifts, her longings, and the quiet, interior nudging of the Holy Spirit. If she later expresses regret over her choice, we help her focus on what had gone into the *process* of deciding rather than on her choice of soccer.

Kids can and should learn to consider two things as they're making significant decisions: Where is this desire coming from, and what is my intention in the action I've chosen? Desires, after all, can be rooted in hunger for pleasure or thirst for power, or even in the more noble love of humanity. But by our mentoring, adolescents can come to recognize those more authentic desires that spring from Christ's Spirit.

For example, eighth-grader Yumiko came home from high school orientation, excited about all of the options for student activities she had just seen. She heard presentations by the service club, foreign language club, student council, and many others, but she told her dad she's most interested in trying out for cheerleading.

Yumiko's co-discerning father invited her to look at the source of her desire and the intention behind her choice. If her desire springs from *hunger for pleasure*, she might say something like this: "I think cheerleaders look awesome, Dad. Their uniforms are cool, and they get to wear them every time there's a game. Cheerleaders get to date all the good-looking guys, and I'd get to go to all the best parties." Dad might be tempted to stop the conversation right there and nix the whole idea. And maybe padlock her in her bedroom for the next four years.

If Yumiko's decision is rooted in *thirst for power*, on the other hand, her response will be somewhat different: "Dad, I was always on the outside in middle school. I hated it. Nothing I could do would make the kids see me as cool. This is my chance to start over, Dad. I could finally have respect." For the bleeding heart dad, this would be enough to convince him that cheerleading is indeed a good choice for his daughter. Another branch of the same dynamic of power might bring these words from Yumiko: "I want to rule the school, Dad. I want to be so high on the social ladder that I can hurl rotten lemons at all those kids who kept me down in middle school." That one's a little easier for Dad to discern.

But Yumiko's father might be pleasantly surprised to hear this from his daughter, based on that charming *love of humanity* she has always displayed: "Dad, I want to support the athletes in my new school. They work so hard with all those practices and everything. We get to decorate their lockers before every game. Think how much that will mean to them." Yumiko's dad is beaming with pride at the nobleness of her choice.

From a young, impressionable teen, it's not realistic to hope for words like, "Cheerleading will bring me communion with God," or "I believe waving poms can help me radiate the love of Jesus, right corrupt systems, and die to self." But I do remember Doreen Ramirez, a cheerleader I once taught who without ever using pious words spread love and harmony and goodwill among her squad like no one I had ever seen before—simply by her gentle presence and awareness of goodness in others.

If Yumiko's desire has evolved from *Christ's Spirit in her,* her dad will more likely hear something like this: "There's something in me that finds this appealing, Dad. I always feel alive when I dance, as you know, and this is similar. My friends always tell me my enthusiasm is my best quality, and of all my choices of activities, cheerleading is where I can best do that. Besides, I just love people, and this is a good way to meet other kids who share my school spirit." Words expressing that a particular choice makes one feel alive, that it's a reflection of what others see as a gift, and that it's a way of loving are sound indicators that your child is responding to the Spirit's nudge within.

Realistically, Yumiko probably has tidbits of all of the above reasons in the back of her mind. But for her father to help her discern what will bring her life rather than subtle or overt destruction, he will lead her to examine why she's making the decisions she's making. This reflection is a crucial step in the discernment process.

GIVE THE DECISION TIME

When discernment is authentic, certainty grows stronger. If not, certainty dissipates and gives way to other options. Teenagers often find themselves moving along with the current of peer enthusiasm.While their friends can be quite convincing in their advice, time is always on the side of the discerner.

Jorge and his friends were entertaining ideas about homecoming. By the time he arrived home, Jorge had his hand on the phone, ready to call the girl all of his friends said he should invite. She liked him; some of his friends were inviting her friends; she would fit into the group. But something stopped him from making the call. The next morning, his enthusiasm had dampened a bit. Something inside didn't feel right. The girl he felt most comfortable with was Megan. They weren't dating yet, but he liked everything about her. As the days went on, inviting his friends' choice didn't feel like the best decision. One evening Megan came into the ice-cream store where Jorge worked. So sure was he by now that he wanted to attend homecoming with her that he ran into the back room and came out with an ice-cream cake. On it were the words, "Will you go to homecoming with me?" When he saw Megan's smile, he felt levity within. A sense of peace about his decision stayed with him through the weeks before the dance. Jorge knew with certitude that he had made the right choice.

BEWARE OF DARKNESS

A co-discerning parent will caution the young person to not make decisions in periods of darkness and, if possible, to avoid changing an authentic discernment during a bleak time. Depression among young people is not at all uncommon and can lead to spiritual and emotional desolation. And for some young women, the menstrual cycle can affect their emotions. A young woman might decide during this time to break up with her boyfriend, abandon a goal she had set for herself, or cancel a trip she had planned, saying it was stupid. Simply noticing that tendency can be very freeing for young women.

No matter how hard we try to buffer our children from pain, adolescence finds a way to pierce them with a vengeance. Sometimes darkness lasts longer than kids have patience for. Parents can offer the stability of co-discernment by encouraging their children to postpone their decision until the light returns. On the spiritual journey, messiness often indicates growth. If our children can't grasp that, we parents can hold onto that hope for them.

Lien helped her daughter through a rough time when Kim was thirteen:

Kim came home sobbing one day from her new school. According to her, all the girls in her class had ganged up on her, and the ringleader was her best friend. She wanted to go back to her old school. I sympathized with her and told her that changing schools wasn't impossible, but that she should wait to make that decision until her anger, fear, and sadness had subsided. As I expected, she was back in the good graces of her friends before the next week.

If Lien had rushed her daughter over to the registration office of her old school that week, she would have modeled for Kim an unhealthy pattern: making decisions in times of darkness. She would also have been denying the authenticity of the decision the family had made the previous spring to enroll Kim in the new school. And finally, she would have robbed Kim of the growing experience of learning how to resolve conflict.

ALLOW YOUR TEENS TO MOVE FORWARD

I remember a trip our family took a few years ago. We were dead tired and heading toward a hotel for a night of rest when we ran into what turned out to be a two-hour traffic jam. Then, just as we got out of the bottleneck, we hit a pothole and flattened a tire. We all talked at length about what we should have done to avoid all this delay, when my son said, "Well, we did our best with the information we had at the time." That wisdom became our motto for the rest of the trip.

After a decision is made in good faith, give the child freedom to move forward and not look back. In discernment, we do our best with the information we have at the time, with the circumstances that present themselves, and with our ability to sense certitude at that particular moment. If, with time, the decision feels wrong to your teen, it would be wise to examine the process with him or her to see where it broke down and to use this information next time. But to spin wheels is a waste of spiritual energy.

LOOK FOR SIGNS OF AUTHENTIC DISCERNMENT

After the young person has made a choice, we would hope to see gladness and a sense of peace. Some degree of certitude should be present, which, although not always strong and clear, should deepen with time. Joseph Tetlow would further suggest that we might witness a more obvious desire for virtue in the context of that decision, such as reaching out in service to others. An increase in trust in God, heightened faith, and hope are other hallmarks of a true discernment. Over time, as our adolescent makes a habit of sound discernment, we should see growth in knowledge of self.

On the other hand, a young person who has discerned poorly will most likely exhibit signs of dis-ease, such as varying degrees of turmoil, depression, or darkness in the wake of her or his choice. She or he may act out or withdraw, display disquiet, withhold eye contact, become cynical around aspects of the particular decision, or become defensive. A teen who makes a poor decision isn't happy about it. Parents will be wise to listen to that inner voice of God's Spirit to discern how the young person is disguising a discernment that doesn't promote her or his spiritual good.

It's helpful to young people to hear us verbalize the qualities that we see in them when they've made a choice that is true and right. As spiritual mentors, we want to help kids build a history of good discernment. Our reminding them of previous good decisions while accompanying them in the current one is a reminder that God is faithful in presence and action.

Similarly, if we are uncomfortable with the results of a child's choice, we have a responsibility to speak up. Yet we need to be discriminating about when and how to speak, for continually raising objections can be habit-forming and not in the best interest of helping kids discern. They will likely not be surprised though when we tell them that instead of peace, love, joy, patience, kindness, generosity, faithfulness, gentleness, and self-control (Gal. 5:22–23), we see signs of disorder within and lack of interior freedom.

To complete the process of co-discerning, we will be with our kids in love and nonjudgment as we review what they've just been through to reach this choice and help them become aware of how the process broke down. Without rescuing them, we help them pick up the pieces and move on to more successful experiences of discernment.

WHEN TO DISCERN

It's not necessary to use the spiritual gift of discernment with every choice our children make. Obviously, whether Brittany invites Maria or Courtney to her ball game is not worth the time it takes to go through the process of discernment. Nor is it particularly significant whether Phan chooses the striped T-shirt or the plain one.

However, what makes this process successful is using the language of discernment often and in a variety of scenarios. This practice brings to our children's awareness the omnipresence of God, even in the seemingly insignificant. From early on, we can make such casual comments as "Are you glad you decided to invite Maria? That was a good choice, huh?" or "You wear that T-shirt almost every day. You made a good decision to buy it." Similarly, we can share such observations as "There's something in your voice that sounds like you would rather invite Maria this time. Am I right? Then that's who you should invite, sweetheart."

Using the language of discernment from early on gives us hope that God's wisdom will stay with our kids when they choose to rove on their own. Although disconcerting to parents, exploration, even in faith matters, is a normal and healthy part of human development. A man who took part in a parenting study group shared his worry that neither of his children felt very strongly about the faith he loved so much. In fact, they rolled their eyes every time he tried to talk about God in their lives. How could he help them discern if they were closed to spirituality?

No pat answers to this question. As parents we must be discerning about what to say and when to say it. We can successfully guide our kids in decision making using the principles of discernment simply because it benefits them. That *is* something kids will embrace. Our young folks are on their own path, and God is in charge. We give them the language of faith and the tools for discernment, and it will connect in a faith perspective in God's time.

Helping kids discern does not result in a passive, laissez-faire model of parenting. On the contrary, it's an active and interactive practice, requiring energy and attentiveness. We are still their primary experience of God at this age. Our message, like God's, is that we'll be with them through it all.

Chapter 5

CO-DISCERNING PARENTS IN ACTION

MY FINGERS flew across the keyboard as I tried to keep up with the instant messages my son and I were batting back and forth from half a continent apart. Nineteen-year-old Andrew, in his first year of college in Pennsylvania, was in a quandary.

"It's not that I don't like it here, Mom. I've done some incredible things I never would have done if I had stayed in Colorado. But at this school I feel like kind of an outsider. The other students talk about 'just getting through this class,' but I'm looking for some intellectual stimulation. I'm thinking about transferring to a small liberal arts college in Oregon."

"Is that right?" I responded, hoping the same reverence I awarded the adults I saw in spiritual direction would translate through cyberspace. He deserved that respect; his dilemma was just as important to him as theirs were to them.

But the more pragmatic part of me began to buzz, and I found myself swatting away typical parental thoughts: What do you know about this other school? We haven't even visited it. Do they offer your major? Financial aid is going to be nearly impossible to get at this late date. You can't keep flitting from college to college. Your school has a good reputation; don't ruin your chances for a good job by throwing this one out. Why not just come home and reapply for that scholarship to the Colorado college you turned down last spring?

But I kept my thoughts locked securely inside.

"I don't know, Andrew," I typed thoughtfully. "Something's not fitting for me."

"Well, it's fitting for me," he countered defensively.

I had taught him too well.

"So, tell me what you're thinking." I grabbed my wrists and peeled my fingers off the keyboard before I said more than I should.

"When I say this, don't get me wrong," he continued. "I'm glad I have options. But sometimes all the choices are overwhelming. Take this college, for instance. I'm an environmental science major, but my school's administration isn't very environmentally conscientious. People on campus don't seem to really care either. In fact, the whole city seems stubborn about it. So in that way, this college feels wrong for me.

"On the other hand, maybe I can grow from this. Maybe this is my opportunity to learn to listen to other people's points of view and accept them where they are."

I gulped. How did this child get so mature?

I didn't want to waste time with anything inane, so I pecked out the words, "Say more!" and pounded the enter key.

"If I go to Oregon, I think I'll meet people more like myself. But I can't decide if that's the easy way out, or if my growth in that setting would be to become more informed and firmer in my views. But if I stay here, I can get a respected degree and maybe make a difference in the world because of that."

Truly, I was dumbfounded by his wisdom. I also realized what a sacred place I was in at that moment—as his mother, as a mentor, as a listener-to-the-heart. I was on holy ground. I slipped my shoes off and pushed them under the desk.

Our computer conversation continued: "I think of those times recently when I felt like I was in the right place. When I protested with the homeless at the inauguration in January. When I camped out in New York last month to protest energy waste. I felt at home. Like this is where I really belonged."

My fingers were twitching now. It was time to respond to my seeker in Pennsylvania.

"That's it, Andrew. That's the feeling you want to look for. If it feels true and right for you, that's how you know you're making the right decision."

"Aaaaaaaah," splashed the blue word onto my screen.

"Listen to those feelings," I continued. "You don't need to deliberately surround yourself with people who think differently from you." Not at this age anyway, I thought. "You have a lot to learn from people who share your same values. And I can guarantee that life will give you plenty of opportunities to learn to accept other people's differences—even while you're immersed in people who are supposedly just like you.

"The interesting thing about this decision you're trying to make, Drew, is that it's not a question of one being right and the other wrong. Good will come out of either choice, don't you think? It's more a question of what is more life-giving for you.

"No matter what decision you end up making, listen for that feeling of peace. That feeling of 'this feels right.' And don't be surprised if you end up opting for the choice you're less inclined to make right now. It happens all the time. The real question is, 'Is this true and right for me?' "

CO-DISCERNMENT IN ACTION

It aches to hear a beloved young adult agonizing over a choice. Yet when our kids include us in their decisions, we have a golden opportunity to guide them to spiritual and emotional maturity. The surest path to such wholeness is to follow what Joseph Tetlow calls God's *hope* for us. Just as a spiritual director listens closely to his or her directee, helping that person to listen closely to and act on the stirrings of God's Spirit within, so, too, must parents recognize this kind of listening as the most sacred work they do for their children. In a spiritual sense, parents have the awe-filled role of being co-discerners of God's hope for their teens. This is co-discernment *in action*.

Like God, we also have magnanimous hopes for our youth. When my parent-child retreat team gives family retreats, we begin by asking parents, "What do you want most for your child?" Typical answers include "I want my youngster to know God's love and presence," "I want her to be happy," "I want him to be emotionally healthy and spiritually whole," "I want him to always have a sense of hope," and "I want her to love herself." It seems a universal desire that we want our young folks to know the fullness of life that God has in mind for them. And we have the opportunity to accompany them on that journey.

God's hope for our kids, if they only knew about it, is one they would buy into with enthusiasm. One of my parenting role models, a woman who has raised four happy, healthy, self-directed young adults, once gave this advice: "I think the key is to let them know we're on their side." If our role is to help our kids discern what will truly bring them life and freedom from those choices that are possibly destructive, what better way is there than to let them know actively and continuously that God is on their side?

A wall hanging that graces a friend's living room reads: "Children are not things to be molded, but people to be unfolded." Parents are partners with God in this sacred unfolding. As co-discerners, parents have the privilege of walking side by side with their teenagers, as they unfold into all that God intends them to be: confident, emotionally healthy, free, spiritual beings. We support our young people in this shared vision. This is the essence of our vocation to raise families.

HONOR DEEP YEARNINGS

Co-discerning means vigilantly seeking God's presence and action in the very fabric of our youngsters' lives. To this end, discernment is not compatible with a God's-will-versus-my-will mentality. I listened to a homily once when the impassioned deacon exhorted the congregation to be vigilant about asking, "Is this God's will [he pointed up to the sky] or my will [he pointed downward]?" He delivered this supplication a half-dozen times in the course of his sermon, and it disturbed me. A sincere follower of what I discern to be God's hope for me and for my family, I would never disagree that the heart of our decisions must always be just that: a sincere desire to follow God's will. What disturbed me was the implication that if it's my will, I should be suspicious that it's not God's will. Why the dichotomy?

If we conscientiously raise our children with a strong moral code, then what do we risk by suggesting that their deepest longings have been planted in their hearts by

God, who dwells within? If we are by their side and on their side as they discern, certainly we have a unique opportunity to encourage ideas that are life-giving, pointing out that these are from God, and that the hallmarks of this choice are peace and certitude. Hundreds of souls would have been exposed to healthy spirituality that day if the homilist had explained discernment in this way rather than with a dire warning that we'd better beware of our ideas and desires.

Co-discerning parents listen to the deep longings of their teenagers' hearts and to the physical demeanor that accompanies them. During her teenage years, my daughter Anne grew in deep affinity to people who experienced life as oppressive: poor people, homeless people, single mothers, battered women, people with racial differences. In her research, she also became disillusioned with the people who helped create and prolong this injustice.

When it came time for Anne to apply for jobs, she was approached by someone in the mall who invited her to work for his popular clothing store because she was "just the kind of person" that store wanted as an employee. Anne was dragging by the time she returned home.

"Can you believe it, Mom?" she asked incredulously. "That man only wanted me because, by appearances, I'm the stereotypical American teenager. I'm not going to promote that image for him. Everyone's so white, you have to wear sunglasses in his store. And some of the brands he carries are made in sweatshops. In fact, I can't see myself working at the mall at all, but that seems to be where all the jobs are."

Several weeks later, she and I participated in a fundraising walk for a nearby safe house for battered women.

I watched in amazement as her whole demeanor changed. She looked around in awe. Her eyes were bright and clear as she listened to the speakers. Her whole body was energized, when suddenly she turned to me and said, "I absolutely love it here. These people are so real."

I encouraged Anne to trust those feelings that had emerged during the walk and to see where they would lead her. She had tapped a deep longing, and the Spirit was nudging her toward fulfillment of that desire in accordance with her gifts.

Anne ended up doing volunteer work at a women's shelter to feed her soul, while working as a lifeguard to feed her coffers.

Back to Andrew and his college quandary. The decision he came to several weeks after our conversation was to stay where he was for another year. That summer, he would visit the college in Oregon and see how he felt about it. He felt that if he made a rushed decision, he might regret it later. What's noteworthy is that I hadn't verbalized any such advice. This was his decision. Sometimes, freeing the young person to make his own decision releases that urgent *need* to change the status quo.

The story doesn't end there. The next fall, Andrew called saying he could hardly stand his restrictive environment any longer. He said the words I was dreading most: "I'm thinking about taking a semester off. I feel like I'm on a moving train that's taking me somewhere I don't want to go. I have to get some space and think about this some more." I groaned inside. I know that if a friend told me her young adult was taking this path, I would affirm that choice, knowing that kids eventually find their way.

But this was *my* child, for heaven's sake. Illogically, I wanted to change the rules. My fear was that Andrew would wander aimlessly and never return to college.

In my own discernment, I received the insight that my need for neat, tidy conclusions was the driving force behind wanting him to stay in school. Affirming his decision was the hardest thing I'd ever done. It was, for me, a real test of whether I truly believed what I preached. In the end we, his parents, gave him the freedom to do what felt right for him—a decision that was definitely not what we would have chosen.

But the story doesn't end there either. Andrew completed the paperwork to withdraw from school. He moved forward with his semester exams, content that these would be his last for a while. Then one day, one of his professors got wind that he wasn't returning. Seeing Andrew's potential, as well as his gifts, he asked Andrew, "What can we do to keep you here?" He understood our son in a way that most people couldn't. This man—I embarrass my son by calling him an angel—proceeded to take Andrew under his wing, designed a program that fit Andrew's needs and his unique way of learning, and promised to serve as his mentor for the remaining years. And as if this weren't enough, the offer also included geological exploration and environmental studies in other countries. Andrew was cautiously excited and relieved when he called with this latest development. This surpassed any conclusion to his story that I could have possibly dreamed up.

As I reflect on the miracle of these events—yes, God's work—I'm painfully aware that had we insisted on his staying in school, our son might never have received this gift. I am also humbled, in the best sense of the word, to see how successfully God works through other significant adults. Through this incident, I learned to walk with trust into the mystery of God's ongoing revelation. And I cemented my long-held belief that life has a way of working out.

Actively listening to our kids' minds and hearts, affirming what they're thinking and feeling, and encouraging them to honor their deepest yearnings—these practices of co-discernment empower our emerging young adults to love what is unique about themselves. The love and respect present in families where parents co-discern give honor to our loving God.

Chapter 6

DISCERNMENT AND PEER PRESSURE

IN MY EXPERIENCE with high school students, I see a wide variety of reactions to peer pressure. While some kids appear content with who they are, others seem to constantly seek approval from their peers by conforming to their expectations. Probably more realistic is that *most* young people give in to peer pressure *sometimes.*

Peer *pressure* is exactly that—a force that attempts to push a teen in one direction or another. We can't always predict the final destination.

Out of curiosity I conducted an admittedly unscientific (that is, over cups of tea), demographically biased (that is, wherever we happened to be living at the time) survey of randomly chosen subjects (my friends) over many years (I did that part right). My questions: Why do you think you gave in to peer pressure? Why do you think you didn't?

The results of my study, now ready for publication, are as follows: Not one person said they *never* gave in to peer pressure. Most said their need to conform to their peers' expectations diminished with age and maturity. Quite a few "dids" said they got most of their affirmation from their friends and made a career of doing what they needed to do to keep it. Many "didn'ts" said their parents believed in them, and they wanted to live up to that. Still others said they had no idea why they did or didn't succumb to peer pressure.

This inconclusive study confirms one truth: human nature is variable. It should be no surprise, then, that the approval of peers, and hence peer pressure, assaults some more than others. Yes, even kids who have learned to discern. We have no guarantee that discerning families will be free of peer pressure. But, as in all areas of growth, we do our best to provide our youth with the environment and the tools to stand firm in their truth, and we give them plenty of opportunities to practice.

PARENT-TEEN RAPPORT

Families meet the challenges of contemporary culture when they make thoughtful decisions in an atmosphere of family support. A mother of teenagers remembers the time her seventeen-year-old, Stasha, came home one day excited to share her plan to go camping for a weekend with a group of friends, including her nineteen-year-old boyfriend:

As I look back, I think Stasha had planned exactly how she would ask our permission in order to elicit a yes. She appealed to our belief in her integrity. She knew we would ask her if she felt right about it, and she was ready with her answer. She had thought long and hard, and, yes, she felt good about going. As she predicted, we said yes.

A week later, Stasha came in late from a date. The next morning, her dad and I confronted her. "You know what our rules are, Stasha, and you broke them. We've always trusted you to do what you know is right. We're disappointed."

"Does that mean you're not going to let me go camping with Jake?" Stasha blurted out.

The immediacy of Stasha's question was enormously revealing. My sense was that my daughter didn't, in fact, feel right going camping with her boyfriend, and she was looking for an excuse to say no. We had always told our children that if they needed a reason to say no, they could blame us. But Stasha hadn't claimed that privilege. I suppose she had conflicting feelings: a big part of her probably did want to spend a weekend with Jake. But a quieter, nagging voice was telling her it was not true and right for her. Even so, she couldn't bring herself to tell her boyfriend no. We seized this opportunity to help her illuminate the voice of wisdom that was so obviously trying to break through.

This story illustrates how a history of open communication between parents and children pays off. It's also a powerful testimony to the importance of ongoing discernment. Even though Stasha knew that the decision was truly hers, that her parents were on her side, and that they would help her make a decision that was true and right for her, the pull of loyalty to her boyfriend was stronger, at least momentarily. Because her parents paid attention to the words-behind-the-words when Stasha asked if they were going to ground her for coming home late, they were able to talk it out with Stasha, giving voice to the wisdom that was already within her. Only a few days earlier, kept in darkness, Stasha's inner voice was buried by her more overt romantic desires. Stasha's mother offers one further reflection on this incident:

I wish I could say my husband and I have always handled such peer pressure issues so successfully. Stasha is our second child, and, believe me, we made plenty of mistakes with our first. In a way, I suppose we were ready for this because of the mistakes we had made. The blessing of our errors is the firm belief we now hold to listen to that inner voice and follow it, and to teach our children to do the same.

PARENTS MODELING RESISTANCE

Parents have opportunities to model their own resistance to peer pressure. At a discernment retreat I gave recently for adults, several came up to me afterward, somewhat sheepishly, to admit that they still felt peer pressure at times. Here are some of their laments:

- I was criticized for not letting both daughters enroll in gymnastics teams that would have kept us running three afternoons a week and all day every Saturday. I believe children need spontaneous time as well. So I went against the grain.
- I loved doing Christmas—baking, decorating, and so forth. My children are now adults, and I'm tired of all this activity. But the extended family, my mother-in-law and sisters-in-law especially, expect and nearly demand I continue these traditions. My husband's mother is eighty-three years old now, and my husband and his sisters keep saying she doesn't have that many years left, and they count on me. I feel trapped.
- I feel pressure to be the best mom ever. My friends who are stay-at-home moms like me talked me into joining a mother's group that encourages moms to take their children everywhere with them. When I listen to those women sharing, I get depressed. The truth is I need a break from my kids regularly—as much as I love them. The pressure to conform to this group is too much for me.

How parents resolve their own dilemmas surrounding peer pressure can have a powerful impact on kids. The message that I believe in myself and that I am swayed by nothing other than my own truth, even though it's hard sometimes, is a value as solid as bedrock, as enduring as the mountains.

CULTIVATING SELF-LOVE AND SELF-RESPECT

The family is the most significant community a young person belongs to, and it's the one community that can make it safe for young people to believe in themselves. A woman named Sherri tells how beleaguered she felt each day at school when her classmates constantly made exaggerated gagging gestures when they saw the eczema on her arms. Too often, a child who is not accepted by her peers will do anything to gain their approval. Sherri was ripe for peer pressure. But fortunately, home was a safe haven. Her mother told her she was beautiful, that her kind nature was what was most attractive about her, and that while her eczema would go away, the kindness would always last. In Sherri's ten-year-old mind, that made sense. Believing in herself, in her real gifts, fortified her against the attacks of her peers.

A young man who now admits that he swayed back and forth under the influence of friends for most of his teenage years finally learned—on his own—a valuable lesson:

One day, when I was trying to make a decision, I felt really uneasy because I didn't have anyone to talk it over with. Well, I'll be honest. I was panicking. I always used to do what everyone else thought I should do. But I didn't have any choice this time. I had to decide. So I did, then I worried about it for a week. Some people told me I made the right decision, and others criticized me for it. Then I came to a huge realization: If I had decided in the other direction, I still would have had people tell me I was wrong. I had to go with my best wisdom. Even using that word—wisdom—puts a whole new light on how I see myself.

I really love and admire my dad, but I wish he had taught me differently in one area. He made me think there was a right way of doing something and a wrong way, and I often chose the wrong way, according to·him. What I finally realized is that there are several right ways of doing just about everything. I think if I had grown up knowing that, I might have been more sure of myself.

Thirty-year-old Denise has this to say about the family culture she was raised in:

I didn't rebel when I was a teenager. Some of my friends were sneaking out and doing all kinds of things their parents told them not to do—just to show they could do it if they wanted to, I guess. I'm not sure what was going on in their heads. But I didn't have parent issues. I had nothing to rebel against. My parents believed in me, and I would have felt awful if I had betrayed that trust.

Admittedly, trusting our children with their peers is more difficult for some of us than others. Some parents can be overprotective of kids because they know first-hand what dangers lurk and beckon. Other parents, problem free in their own adolescence, can be overly trusting of their teens. Depending on the circumstance, most of us fall somewhere in between. All parents, therefore, will want to prayerfully discern that balance of trust that empowers kids to grow into their own faith in the discernment process.

I raised children with a gentle neighbor, Toni. While our youngsters played together, we shared our dreams of what they would become. "I admire my husband's parents," she said, "and I would like to raise our children the same way they raised theirs." Pressed further, she explained:

They started out with the premise that they could trust their children. And they didn't change that stance until a child proved untrustworthy. When it was needed, they tightened the reins. Stan and I started dating when we were teenagers, and I always knew him to make mature decisions. I really think the reason he's so healthy is that he felt love and respect from his parents at a crucial age.

Clearly, these twin fruits, self-love and self-respect, don't crop up spontaneously. They are carefully cultivated in a family that makes healthy children, healthy lives a priority. To this end, the only conformity we need encourage is compliance with God's hope for us.

Chapter 7

DISCERNMENT AND PERFECTIONISM

PERFECTIONISM is one of the plagues of adolescence. Indeed, the structure of the teenage environment is rooted in it. Young people are ranked in school, rated on the job, placed into social strata by their peers, often on the basis of external, superficial criteria. They are reminded daily that they're not perfect. Rabbi Harold S. Kushner, in his book *How Good Do We Have to Be? A New Understanding of Guilt and Forgiveness* (Boston: Little, Brown and Company, 1996), goes to great lengths to convince us of the harm we inflict on ourselves with our tendency (adults and teenagers alike) to too often "let ourselves be defined in our own minds by our worst moments instead of our best ones" (p. 38). The resulting shame is so destructive that healing can take years.

ACCEPTING YOURSELF

Discernment can close our youths' ears to the insidious suggestion that there is such a thing as a perfect person, and that they fall short. Discernment can serve as blinders to this invasive culture. Discernment teaches young people that standing in their truth is all the perfection they need, whatever that looks like compared with others.

Caterina, a mother of four, shares this lesson she learned about perfectionism and discernment:

My husband and I had three bright, "normal," achieving children who graduated with honors from the same public high school, went on to college, and now live successful, happy lives. When the youngest of these was sixteen, our family welcomed the birth of our little bonus, Marissa. When Marissa reached middle school, she experienced panic and anxiety about going to school, and by the time she started high school, she was suffering from depression. She asked to switch from the school where her brothers and sisters had been so successful. I found that appalling. She was such a great kid that she should also be a high achiever like her siblings.

Without knowing anything about discernment, I learned the hard way. One day something inside me was finally able to hear her frustration and sense of powerlessness. My husband and I gave her our blessing and enrolled her in a smaller school, where she is a happy, involved senior, and successful—in her own unique way. What I learned about discernment is to listen, listen, and listen some more to what my children are feeling, and to accept that as a manifestation of God's will for them. If I could do it over again, I would encourage them to honor that inner voice as well. But I had to get my own expectations out of the way first. I can see now that perfection isn't what God asks of us.

Of course, we as parents have to believe this ourselves. I hear adult after adult bemoan the fact that all during childhood, they felt that no matter how much they did, it wasn't enough. Men have shared their guilt about having disappointed their fathers. I've known women so hard on themselves that it takes years, even decades, to heal to the point where they can accept themselves as they are.

PERFECTIONIST EXPECTATIONS

Striving for perfection can destroy relationships. Betty received a most poignant insight in prayer after her thirty-year marriage ended in divorce. She shared this painful fruit of her grieving: "I might still be married if I had been true instead of perfect." For her, being the perfect wife meant burying her longings for the sake of peace. On the outside, the marriage appeared collaborative. On the inside, Betty's integrity had died.

No matter what perfectionist expectations were thrust upon us by important people in our lives, it's not too late to raise our children in a more compassionate way. A young mother expressed gratitude to her friend for modeling "the most valuable parenting lesson I ever learned: that my children are different from each other, but each is just fine the way she is." This young woman continued: "Believe it or not, I didn't know that. I thought they all should be the same. To tell you the truth, it takes the burden off me. I can let them be who they are."

It has been said that the greatest source of relationship problems is broken expectations. When we parents hold unrealistically high expectations over our children, not only are we doomed to disappointment, but our children are condemned to a life of low self-esteem. People are simply not perfect. I was humbled many years ago when, out of exasperation, my firstborn finally broke out in a tirade, "You just committed a sin, Mom."

Huh?

"Yeah, you did. You think I'm God, and that's a sin. You want me to be perfect, but I'm not. Only God is perfect." Because I had learned by then that children have a strong sense of justice, I knew to listen to this indignant child. What he said was true. At the time, I thought it was my job as a parent to turn out perfect children. Fortunately, this child set me straight, and I never again implied to my children that they should be flawless. Now, twenty years later, I can brag that we have a family that is perfectly imperfect!

Stored in my knowledge bank are some hazy statistics that soaked in from a parenting talk I attended years ago: virtually all parents say they love their children, but only around half of the children say they feel loved. When we demand perfection from our children, these are the statistics that evolve. Most of us would agree that children aim to please their parents. If they perceive that they have failed, their self-love is eroded.

Again I resort to the words God spoke through the prophet Isaiah:

> I have called you by name: you are mine. . . .
> . . . You are precious in my eyes . . .
>   and . . . I love you.

(Isa. 43:1–4)

That period at the end is significant. God didn't say, "I love you because . . ." or "when you . . ." or "despite the fact that. . . ." Nor did God say, "I would love you if . . ." or "I will love you when . . ." God said, "I love you." In our attempts to free our children from the shackles of perfectionism, we might examine these subtle ways we may be passing on perfectionist attitudes.

Clint, having read an article about the importance of a father's influence in a daughter's success, reflects on how to be a positive power in her life:

When I first learned about a father's role in his daughter's achievements, I took my job very seriously, and I approached it with great zeal. I thought the best way to encourage Tanisha was to discourage behaviors or attitudes that would—from my point of view—impede her. So when she started going to the mall with her friends as a form of entertainment, I told her I would respect her more if she used her time for physically healthy activities like biking or hiking. When she signed up to take a fashion design course at school, I told her that she had what it takes to be a doctor, that I valued her great mind, and that I would admire her for taking a good, solid biology course instead. Then when she abided by my wishes, I would praise her.

In looking back, I realize I was being manipulative. Tanisha was trying to be perfect for me. I would have had a greater impact on her, I think, if I had encouraged her to follow her own dreams, to be true to herself over being true to me.

NOT PERFECTION, BUT INTEGRITY

Discernment is perhaps the strongest shield against perfectionism. Saint Paul wrote to the Ephesians, "Living the truth in love, we should grow in every way into him who is the head, Christ" (4:15). Doing the truth is our invitation to live with spiritual integrity, that is, to act as a whole person, who knows and loves himself or herself. Integrity involves knowing and acknowledging our gifts, being faithful to our call to love, and accepting that we are deeply and unconditionally loved by God.

Kushner, in studying the verse from Gen. 17:1, where God says to Abraham, "Walk in my presence and be blameless" (Hebrew *tamim*), concluded that what God is asking of Abraham and of us is "not perfection, but integrity. God wants Abraham to strive to be true to the core of who he is, even if he strays from that core occasionally" (*How Good Do We Have to Be?* p. 170).

One way we can teach our kids to know their truth is to help them be aware of when they feel interior disorder, a sign that they're resisting their truth. Sins against the

Great Commandment—love of God, neighbor, and self—cause disturbance within. In young people, this interior turmoil may manifest itself as embarrassment, confusion, shame, anger, or angst. But kids can also sit in denial. We parents can often discern children's feelings of shame by looking into their eyes and watching their body language. They may evade our glance, for example. Or we might see them fidgeting, being more loud or quiet than normal, or resisting our hugs. Over time, we can recognize how our individual child tries to disguise shame.

Shame is a by-product of perfectionism. It's a darkness that carries great power if kept out of the light. It separates a person from her or his truest, most whole self, from others, and from God. As parents, we can help our children bring their interior disorder to the surface by talking it out with them and, in so doing, let it disintegrate by God's grace.

An eighty-year-old woman tells this story:

My childhood was marred by the embarrassment of my parents' divorce in a time when divorce was rare and in a town where judgments were harsh. I was thirteen years old at the time, self-conscious, and concerned with what people thought. Even though my mother initiated the divorce out of fear for her safety, she never shared that with me. All I knew was that something was wrong with our family. In truth, my mother was very courageous. Now I can hold my head high as I tell people I love and admire my mother. But at the time I felt alienated from everyone. I was angry at Mother and at God for making my life so imperfect. And I was plagued with shame. I lived in darkness during those years.

Integrity, not perfection. When adversity strikes a family, how much more life-giving it is to provide young people with the tools to say with confidence, "This is my truth: my life is thus and so, but I'm lovable and loved," than to leave them powerless about their own self-worth.

Compare the story above with that of Matt, a young man of sixteen who suffered brain injuries in a biking accident. His road to recovery was long and discouraging and included abandonment by friends, who didn't know what to do. But Matt had an inner integrity that helped him say with confidence: "My life sucks. But I'm not going to let that get in the way of enjoying it." The practice of discernment can instill in our kids an attitude that our truth is not perfection; it is acceptance of what is.

STAND IN YOUR TRUTH

Fifty-year-old Christina tells of an incident that is almost amusing as she reflects on it:

When I was ten, I looked up to my best friend as the model of perfection. Whatever she said was truth. One day she showed me a new crucifix she had received from her aunt. It was yellowish-white, and it glowed in the dark! "Ooh," I said, puckering my face. "That's kind of ugly."

My friend sucked in the maggot-infested air that surrounded my insult. When she regained her composure she lectured me. "That's a sin! God is really mad at you for saying that."

Do you know I carried guilt over that "sin" for eight more years? I was too embarrassed to even confess it to a priest. I was pretty sure I hadn't done anything wrong, in which case the priest might laugh at me. On the other hand, maybe I really had sinned, in which case he might be just as shocked as my best friend.

The darkness that haunted Christina for eight years reared its head because she had an external standard of perfection, dependent on what people told her, rather than an internal system of truth. Her intent was innocent of any blasphemy, but she didn't have the know-how to discern what was authentic.

Our kids are not imperfect; they're human. When they fall short or choose poorly, we can help them examine how they impeded their own freedom, placed themselves in turmoil, or decreased their joy by the choice they made. Jesus dealt with human nature throughout his ministry. His words to the woman whom everyone knew as a sinner, but who showered him with love (Luke 7:36–50), showed an understanding that what she had been doing was causing disorder within her, distancing her from her truest, most whole self. He wanted to lead her to freedom. So he simply said, without condemnation, "Go in peace."

Erin, sixteen years old, remembers the night she and two friends decided to drive to the next city to visit their boyfriends at work. Of course, it was a spur-of-the-moment decision, and she still planned to be home by her curfew, so she didn't see any reason to let her parents know about her change in plans, even though it was a standing rule in the family. She didn't feel too much regret about this decision until she heard the urgent voice on the radio as they drove out of the city: "We repeat. All people outside the city limits should be in their basements. This is a tornado warning. Take shelter immediately."

The girls drove as fast as they could to escape the imminent tornado and screeched to a halt when they arrived at the fast-food restaurant where their boyfriends worked. Hearts pounding and out of breath, they stormed into the restaurant, glad to be safe at last. But the drama wasn't over. The restaurant was without electricity, and the employees and customers were all huddled in the back room waiting out the tornado warning. The girls joined them, waiting two hours until calm returned. Erin never had a chance to notify her parents.

When Erin finally got home, she found her worried father waiting. She poured out her story and the fear that had swept through her while trying to escape the tornado. She admitted the panic she had felt that, had she been hurt, her parents would have had no idea where she was. Perhaps out of relief that his daughter was safe more than from a supernatural ability to think about the advantages of helping his daughter discern, Erin's dad spoke calmly: "Can you see the turmoil you caused yourself, Erin? When you make a decision about traveling so far next time, do what's going to bring you peace." A simple approach, but it was an opportunity to tap into Erin's own sense of truth rather than defer to external parameters of perfection.

LAUGH AT YOURSELF

Another way to teach children to stand in their truth and defy perfectionism is to show them how to laugh at themselves by, first of all, learning to laugh at our own selves.

When we believe we should be perfect and then fall short, we often take ourselves too seriously, and those shameful feelings grab hold. But when we can find a way to laugh at ourselves, shame loosens its grip. My friend Mary Ann learned at a young age to make light of her nose, claiming lightheartedly that she and a famous movie star bore a striking resemblance because they had the same "big nose." Truth is, Mary Ann is strikingly beautiful, but she has made a lot of people laugh as she laughed at herself. A student in a neighboring classroom responded to his teacher's request that he straighten up his behavior by saying playfully: "I'm sorry, ma'am. I guess my mom is right. I'm just a regular ball of fire." His tone and demeanor were frolicsome rather than disrespectful, and clearly he had figured out how to laugh at his penchant for hyperactivity so that his ego wasn't defeated by years of being scolded by teachers.

Freedom from perfectionism through discernment brings another benefit. Young people who are not slaves to perfectionism appear to have an easier time letting other people be who they are, whether it's their friends and peers, their romantic interests, or people in society who are different from them. Having learned to "do the truth in love" themselves, all they expect of others is that they live their own truth and live it in love.

Chapter 8

DISCERNMENT AND FRIENDSHIPS

THE THREE OF US were lined up at the mirror like dancers, arms curved gracefully in front of us in exactly the same position. I sneaked a side-glance at my two middle school daughters, trying to get a few tips from them about applying mascara. Suddenly one of them blurted out, "Mom, how can we be popular?"

Now there's a question I had no idea how to answer. My thoughts floated back forty years to my own adolescent years, when I channeled a good deal of energy into the same quest. I attempted to be funny, I tweaked my personality, I tried out for cheerleading, I laughed raucously, and I strove to look like the girl on the cover of *Seventeen*. I even tried just being myself, because that was the wisdom of mature peers and adults. Nothing worked. My friends and I remained forever on the lower echelon of the social stratum. I have to admit, though, that I still had a great time.

I took my daughters' question seriously and prayed for a response that would be in harmony with God's hope for them. "Well," I ventured, "that depends. If being popular means being cool, you don't have a fighting chance. Look at Dad and me. You've inherited nothing but dominant dork genes. On the other hand," I mused, "when I think about the popular people I know, they have one thing in common: they seem interested in me, they're kind to me, they value me, they support me. *I* feel good about *myself* when I'm with them. I didn't know this when I was your age, but I think popularity has more to do with genuinely liking people—and letting them know it—than with how I look or act or what activities I participate in."

"Oh," was about all the girls could say. It wouldn't take them long to discover, if they hadn't already, the hard truth that some kids simply have that nebulous chemistry that exudes "coolness"—and the rest of us don't. The advice I gave my daughters was perhaps more about adult popularity. In the meantime, though, I hoped that kindness would be at the heart of their friendships.

Discernment is germane to friendship in several ways. It empowers teenagers to choose friends who are true and right for them. It helps them recognize that a gnawing inside may be a signal that a relationship is wrong for them. Even in healthy friendships, that same gnawing can inform them when some aspect of the relationship is amiss. Discernment enables young people to set boundaries where needed. Later, when romance enters the picture and judgment can be murkier, teenagers who have been discerning all along with their parents' guidance have a solid foundation for making decisions about love.

FAMILY AFFIRMATION

One of my earliest memories is of my best friend, Gianeen, and me paging through the Montgomery Ward catalog and choosing our favorite outfit on each page. Gianeen was so sure of herself. I found myself thinking more about which one Gianeen was choosing than about which one I really liked. In my mind, there was a right choice and a wrong choice, and Gianeen's was right. As much as I tried to get her to choose first, she sometimes made me go first. When she inevitably chose a different ensemble,

I doubted myself even more. Gianeen and I played this game countless times, as miserable as it was for me, but I persevered for one reason only: some day we would make the same choices, and I would finally know I was okay.

I've thought many times about this childhood dynamic, and of this friend whom I always referred to as the boss in our relationship, wondering why some kids are so confident while others constantly waffle. Where did Gianeen get such a strong sense of self? Someone of importance was surely affirming her. I recall one conversation—we were only ten at the time—when Gianeen said: "You're school-smart, Maggie. But I'm home-smart." She was exactly right! I did well academically, but when it came to practical matters, I had little common sense. Gianeen, on the other hand, could tackle all issues outside of school—in spades—and I was there to tag along, in awe of her brilliance. To this day, she's highly successful at a career for which I don't have a trace of talent. But now, forty years later, I can say that's okay because I have different gifts.

A family that discerns makes a habit of affirming children. The kids see, modeled before them, a dynamic among people that says, "Our opinions are different, not right and wrong." They hear the echo of Saint Paul's Body of Christ message: We each have gifts, and no one's gift is greater or less than yours. When a decision takes them where they don't want to go, instead of disparaging comments like, "You blew it," they hear: "Let's pick up the pieces and move forward. I'll be at your side." With that kind of support at home, young people have the freedom to see themselves authentically. They become equipped with tools for making healthy decisions around friendship.

Considering the time teens spend with friends, we want to give them the strongest foundation at home that we can. Then, as one mother said: "I pray, then sit back and let God work in my children's heart. I have to get out of the way of the Holy Spirit." Helping our children develop an inner sense of truth, an inner sense that God is leading, is the best way to "get out of the way of the Holy Spirit." More accurately, it is the surest way to give the Holy Spirit access to the chambers of our children's souls.

Tomas helped his eleven-year-old daughter Karina recognize when her relationship with a group of girls in the neighborhood was no longer life-giving:

One day Karina came home upset, saying the neighborhood girls had turned against her. I was furious. I had made the mistake when my older daughter Tara was that age of forbidding her to play with her friend who had been mean to her. In fact, I tore her friend apart with my words, I was so mad. I shouldn't have done that. This time, though, I wanted to see if I could support Karina in discovering what was right for her. I let her talk. After hearing the history of her friendship with these girls, I asked her if she saw a pattern. She's a smart kid. She observed that there was a key player in all this who needs to be in control and in the center, and will pull people to her and against others to achieve this. I didn't have to say anything negative about this girl. Karina already saw her for what she was. And I didn't have to forbid her from seeing the girl. Karina knew she had better friends.

OUT OF SYNC

Sometimes a friendship is healthy, but out of sync. Discernment can be the instrument to set the relationship right again. Jeff recalls a time when he knew something was wrong between him and his best friend:

Cory and I had been buds since we were little kids. We got along because we liked all the same things. He was funny, too. He used to tell me stuff he wouldn't tell anyone else, so I guess our friendship had depth, at least more than my other friendships. Now we're in a band together, getting ready to make a CD, so we see each other even more. But it's not like it was before. We're not enemies at all, but it's different. I'm kind of quiet, and Cory is really popular. He doesn't laugh and talk with me like before. I don't know. Maybe that's just the way things are. I might talk to him about it. And I might not.

Notice Jeff isn't ready to abandon the friendship, nor does he feel less about himself because Cory's social circle has enlarged, in contrast to his own. By talking to Cory, he might discover something that would be helpful to their relationship. On the other hand, as so many people with whom I meet for spiritual direction have discovered, relationships change. We have a choice. We can abandon the friend out of hurt, anger, or confusion, or we can redefine the friendship. Jeff seems to grasp that truth. He has discerned a change in the friendship, but he is able to accept the shift once he determines that nothing else is operative in the distancing.

Young people need to learn the importance of setting boundaries with friends. Monique was happy when Chad invited her to prom. He was a friend, part of a large group who hung out together, so it would be comfortable. They talked more than usual before the big event, and Monique found herself enjoying his company. They had a great time at the prom. Afterward, Chad began calling Monique frequently.

Monique reflects on that period of time:

I liked Chad and everything, but I just wanted to be friends. Pretty soon he was calling every day, and I just didn't have that kind of time to be talking to him. One day he called, all excited about a song he had written. It was about me! That was too much. Instead of being flattered, I felt yukky inside. Something felt weird about the whole thing.

I struggled a lot about what to do. I didn't want to destroy the friendship, and I didn't want to say anything hurtful, but I needed to let Chad know he was heading in the wrong direction. I prayed for several days for the right words. After I talked to Chad, I felt at peace with the conversation. It has been a month now, and Chad hasn't called. He might be hurt, but I have to trust that the words that came to me were the right words at the time. Otherwise, I'll drive myself crazy.

SUPPORT FOR FRIENDS

Discerning teens have the tools to support their friends who are making big decisions, including the insight to recognize when a friend is struggling with interior disorder. Often their peers will gravitate toward them, lending credence to the spiritual maturity that discernment has given them.

Miguel was such a person. Intuitive and caring, he sensed that his girlfriend—despite her usual gregarious behavior—was struggling with something, but she didn't want to talk about it. He had to get the dreaded question off his chest: "Are you thinking about breaking up with me?" The resounding no reassured him, so he backed away and let her feel her feelings. Within a month, she shared her burden with Miguel. He listened and empathized, helped her sort out her options, but didn't try to fix it. She had a decision to make, and he supported her as she did.

A word of caution here: teens are still children. They don't have the training of a therapist, the experience to recognize complexities, nor the maturity to always be able to separate themselves from the intricate emotions their friends may be experiencing. They need support. If we as parents sense that our child is involved in something over his or her head, we would be wise to offer the support of co-discernment.

Finally, teenagers who discern have the potential to be valuable friends because they don't hold expectations over others. One of the primary sources of conflict in relationships is broken expectations. Discerning teens let their friends be who they are.

Of course, parents will need to model acceptance. It can be as simple as verbalizing admiration for a friend in the face of his or her obvious shortcomings. Our family has coined a phrase that we use when those flaws get in the way of our wholeheartedly admiring someone: "Well, it's part of his charm!" Acceptance can be as simple as a husband and wife affirming each other for their very differences. I remember overhearing my friend's mother tell her husband: "I'm fascinated with the things you like, honey. I keep thinking how much richer I am because you've introduced me to what you're interested in." Perhaps the most credible example of acceptance is honoring each family member's uniqueness. When a teenager gratefully embraces his or her own individuality, it's a short step to enjoying and supporting the uniqueness of friends.

Our words, according to James, are as mighty as the spark that sets a huge forest ablaze (3:5). Indeed, "From the same mouth come blessing and cursing" (v. 10). Friendships can be defined by affirmation or criticism. They come out of the same mouth. When our teens choose friends, resolve differences, and set boundaries based on an attitude of respect, their words have the power to release the fire of the Spirit's gift of love. Friendships rooted in authentic love are the healthy ones.

Chapter 9

DISCERNMENT AND SEXUALITY

WHAT TEENAGERS do with their sexuality may be their parents' greatest fear. Sexuality is certainly one of the most important issues of adolescence, one parents pray they can address with skill and wisdom. We can all probably agree that the following approaches, though sometimes hard to resist, aren't the best ways to help our adolescents discern God's will in relation to sexuality: Closing our eyes and hoping it'll go away. Shouting out in our fear and frustration, "Don't you dare, do you hear me?" Vacillating between a you-can-talk-to-me-about-anything stance and an unconscious I-hope-you-don't-talk-to-me-about-everything stance.

Not that desperate tactics don't have an impact—at least temporarily. My friend Valerie admitted she simply couldn't come up with a calm, mature, tactful way to broach the subject of chastity when her daughters started dating. One evening as the girls were both getting ready for dates, Valerie stood at the door of the bathroom wringing her hands and moaning, "Girls, if you start having sex, I'll have a nervous breakdown." Indeed, several years later, one of those daughters, by then in college, told me: "I could never move in with my boyfriend. My parents would kill me."

As one mother drove her son to the airport for college, she admonished him about respecting women: "If I ever hear you've been taking advantage of a girl, you'll see my tortured face in your dreams."

Still another neighborhood friend once said: "Shelly's in college now, and I have no idea what she's doing. It's better for my mental health."

Ultimately we have to let go. But before we do, it would no doubt be wise and responsible to equip our soon-to-be young adults with a sound sense of sexuality upon which to make healthy decisions. If we send our kids into life without a strong value system based on love of self and love of others, we are doing them a grave injustice. If we fill them with fear and guilt as a means to control their sexual urges, then we have eroded that self-love that is the foundation of healthy sexuality.

SEXUALITY—A DRIVE TO CONNECT

Adolescents and preadolescents need to see the big picture, what sexuality means for them as whole people. In a chapter entitled "A Spirituality of Sexuality" from his book *The Holy Longing: The Search for a Christian Spirituality* (New York: Doubleday, 1999), Ronald Rolheiser explores the "all-embracing intent of our sexuality" (p. 206), which might serve as a good starting point for fostering a mature attitude about sexuality in our youth. This "intent of our sexuality" involves an awareness of having been disconnected from the whole and our subsequent search to reconnect with another person.

Rolheiser says, "Sex is the energy inside of us that works incessantly against our being alone" (p. 195). It is essential that our youth understand that sexuality and "genitality" are not the same, and that focusing on the latter can make healthy, mature expression of the former nearly impossible. We parents need to delineate between the two as we talk with our teens. Moving directly to a discussion of genital sex as if that were the whole story gives our kids the wrong impression of what we, and God, truly desire for them.

This desire to connect is a force to be reckoned with, even for adults. As with many tendencies, it is stronger in some than in others, but few are true loners. When I accompanied my newly widowed mother to her first grief group meeting, I heard the sadness in the voice of Carl, a man entering his second year alone: "What I miss most is having someone to talk to. Sylvia and I used to drive into the country on Sundays and talk all afternoon." This connective energy also compels recently divorced people to move into new relationships before they've healed. It can be painful to be alone.

In my spiritual direction practice, issues surrounding sexuality are among the most difficult for adults to discern. So imagine how hard discernment must be for adolescents, especially if they have not been equipped with an authentic representation of sexuality. Kids watch as their friends pair up for homecoming and sweetheart dances. No matter how sure of themselves the left-outs appear to be, this in-your-face message surely imprints itself deep within. They crave a connection, and they don't have one. To this void, add their friends' perceptions of what sexuality is, and our kids may be confused about what it is they crave.

God's voice can be overpowered by the strength of this drive to connect. Predictably, adolescents need us to walk by their side as they develop an ear for God's direction among the turbulence of the legendary "raging hormones."

CO-DISCERNING WITH OUR TEENS

The stormy nature of romance provides a strong rationale for being co-discerning parents. Teenagers who first love themselves and respect others, then seek connections that foster this love and respect, have an advantage over those who fall into relationships looking to plug the emotional dike that is making them feel empty and incomplete.

A father expressed concern over his fifteen-year-old daughter, Melissa:

Even though she's not allowed to date until she's sixteen, Melissa always has to be "going out" with someone. She's been doing this since she was twelve. I'm worried about her because she jumps from one relationship to another, always proud that she has a boyfriend. I finally said: "Melissa, having a boyfriend doesn't make you who you are. You have value all by yourself. You're lovable, Mel. You don't need to have a boyfriend to prove that." I don't know if it'll have any effect on her, but I knew I needed to say it. I'm looking for ways now to affirm her as a whole person to counteract this tunnel vision she seems to have picked up from her friends.

Once kids realize that the heart of sexuality is a movement toward connection, they are ready to discern which connections are life-giving and which are not, which nourish and which exploit. Which relationships lead to a fuller communion with God as evidenced by the fruits of peace, love, and joy? And which ones lead to darkness, pleasure seeking, or abuse of power? I repeat Ronald Rolheiser's wisdom that sexuality encompasses far more than "genitality." Physical sexual expression will be empty and unhealthy if it is not cemented in true sexuality: that complete energy that encompasses "love, community, communion, family, friendship, affection, creativity, joy, delight, humor, and self-transcendence" (p. 195).

Carlotta, a forty-five-year-old mother of two, recalled her dating experiences as a teenager:

By the time I started dating, I had been exposed to four years of dire warnings from my parents about the sin of premarital sex. I was ready for whatever might come my way. I was always on the lookout for sexual advances, and made sure I kept a certain emotional distance so the guys wouldn't think I was coming on to them. I heard that one of my dates had said I was cold, which made me pretty proud, considering what they were saying about some of the other girls.

When I went away to college, I felt that my values were pretty well intact. But one night I got carried away with a guy I liked a whole lot. We kissed a lot and that was all, but I felt horrible afterward. I called my best friend from high school and confessed what I had done. She told me she couldn't see what was wrong with what I had done. She said that in her view, physical affection was part of a bigger picture that comes naturally when you like or love the whole person you're with. Her answer shocked me. I thought she was dead wrong, and only years later did I understand her wisdom.

What I realize after all this time is that I missed out on a lot of healthy romances because I was so focused on genital shame that I failed to connect with the heart, mind, and spirit of the person I was with.

Seventeen-year-old Travis shared a different experience:

My mom and dad were teenagers in the 70s. I know for a fact that they had sex before marriage. My youth group director spends one whole night every year telling us to stand up for chastity. But my parents never say anything. I guess they're embarrassed or don't want to be hypocritical or something. I have girlfriends, and I haven't done anything yet, but I really wonder where my parents come from on this. Who knows? Maybe I'll ask them.

What Travis might hear could surprise him. So many of those who got caught up in the sexual revolution have powerful wisdom to pass on to their children. Most will admit that they didn't understand the total picture of sexuality at the time. Some might spread the same wisdom that Maureen felt compelled to share:

What I was reacting to in the 60s was the sexual repression that just wasn't making sense to me. It was like the pendulum was way over on the suppression end, and I hopped on and rode it to the other extreme. I can't say I didn't feel free. I did. I convinced myself that having sex without any limits was quite liberating. But I didn't feel satisfied. I didn't feel whole. I didn't feel centered. Now that I know what real love is, I wouldn't trade it for all the "liberation" in the world. In fact, I've been single for ten years now, and I've remained celibate the whole time. It kind of throws the guys I've dated, but it's amazing what you can find out about someone when sex isn't in the way to cloud it.

Whatever our early sexual experiences, they can hold richness for our children if we pass on the insight we gained from them. Kept in the darkness, on the other hand, they take on a life that fills the air with disquiet, which our teenagers may sense, but not understand.

ONE YOUNG COUPLE'S STORY

Of course, our kids are not always open with us about what's going on in their heads and in their lives, which confirms the need to hold them always in our prayer.

Courtney and Kevin have been dating for two years, since they were sophomores in high school. They courageously shared their story with their youth group not, they said, because they had it all together in the area of sexuality but because they had struggled and felt they had grown because of it:

Courtney: Kevin and I liked everything about each other right from the start. We were alike in most ways, and our parents approved of our relationship. Kevin had had another girlfriend, but this was the first romantic relationship for me. I used to stare at him from across the classroom and wish, wish, wish that he would ask me out. When he finally did, I was ecstatic.

Kevin: Yeah, Courtney couldn't see that I was giving her all kinds of signals, I guess. But it made me feel good that she was excited about going out with me. It was pretty cool the way we got along. I wanted to be with her all the time.

Courtney: Kevin and I were really close. I felt unbelievably lucky to have such a great boyfriend. There was a real warmth to our connection. My friends were jealous that I had someone to go out with, go to all the dances and stuff. I have to admit, I liked the envy. But I also loved all the long talks we had, exploring different interests together, just having fun.

Kevin: After we had been going out for maybe about six months, we started to get physical. I just loved Courtney so much that all I wanted to do was . . . well . . . make love to her. She was kind of straitlaced in that way, so I didn't force anything. But it was killing me. I just wanted Courtney in the worst way.

Courtney: Well, I'm glad he saw it that way! I was feeling the same way, but I didn't let on because I didn't want anything to happen. One of us had to be strong. But one night we had a talk and convinced each other that the fact that we wanted it so badly must be a sign that we should do it. It was so tiring trying to fight it all the time.

Kevin: So for a few months, we let go. I can't say I didn't like it, but something started growing inside both of us that bothered us. We had to talk about it.

Courtney: We didn't like how we were feeling during this period of time. It wasn't as warm and fun as it used to be. It seemed like the physical part had taken on so much importance that the reasons we were attracted to each other in the first place didn't seem to be there anymore.

Kevin: I loved Courtney, but a voice inside was telling me that I was on the wrong path. That was weird, and I knew I could never explain it to my friends. They would just laugh at me. But if I were to admit the truth to myself—which I finally did—I really didn't want our relationship to be so focused on sex.

Courtney: Kevin and I aren't psycho-religious or anything like that, but we do pray. We felt such peace after we changed our way of relating that we both agreed this was God's plan for us.

In co-discerning with our adolescents, we're helping them establish a history of healthy choices surrounding sexuality. And like it or not, this history may include—and be stronger for—the mistakes kids make. Like our God who is with us through it all, co-discerning parents stand with their children even in the mistakes and help them find the path that is most life-giving. If they tell us about it, that is.

Chapter 10

DISCERNMENT AND CHANGE

MOMENTS of change and transition in family life, particularly for youth, provide opportunities for growth. Sadly, though, dramatic change for ten- to nineteen-year-olds is often traumatic. Mental health professionals talk about resiliency in children, and the enigma as to why some children bounce back while others are defeated in the face of change. As Joan Lunden says in her book *Wake-up Calls: Making the Most out of Every Day (Regardless of What Life Throws You)* (New York: McGraw-Hill, 2001), it can take a lifetime to realize that while "change is inevitable, suffering is optional" (p. 105). An end is always a beginning.

Parents of ten- to nineteen-year-olds are generally in midlife, a notorious time of transition. This is the time when a career might take a turn, sometimes necessitating a move; when physical shifts begin to occur; when one parent or the other suffers discontent or depression, resulting in changing family dynamics.

The very fabric of teen life, too, brings about change. Moving from elementary to middle school and then to high school brings new friends, new courses, new jobs, new activities, new choices—a whole new life. For some, the challenges are welcome; for others, frightening.

What helps youth rebound from change, painful or not, is a grounding in the theology that God is with them through it all, guiding them from within toward fullness of life. As parents, our role during times of transition is to help our children discover that change can bring us to a higher level of integrity. Change can clarify our values. As we empower our teens to successfully negotiate change, we can watch them grow confident in their truth.

CHANGE HAPPENS, BUT SUFFERING IS OPTIONAL

Anyone who has been hit square in the face with unexpected change knows that even for mature adults, change can be as shattering as any natural disaster. At worst, the ground upon which we had planted our physical, emotional, and spiritual selves for nearly a lifetime can shift with the fierceness of an earthquake, cracking our very foundation, forcing us to leave our cherished home and start anew. None of us will get through life with the same proverbial rug beneath us. Change is inevitable.

But suffering is optional, and children will look to us for the stability a discerning spirit offers. The inevitability of change is a powerful incentive to become a discerning adult and to get an early start on teaching kids to discern.

Jesus imparted spiritual truth and wisdom to his disciples throughout his time with them. He was their rock. When it was time for him to leave, he acknowledged that they would be overcome with grief, that they would "weep and mourn" (John 16:20). At first they didn't understand the magnitude of the change that lay ahead. But Jesus knew, so he fortified them with the spiritual tools they would need to move forward and breathe life into the Kingdom as he had. He promised them the Advocate, his Spirit, to infuse them with spiritual gifts, including discernment, that would transform this unsettling change into abundant life: "When [the Spirit of truth] comes, . . . he will guide you to all truth. . . . He will glorify me, because he will take from what is mine and declare it to you" (John 16:13–14).

And the best news of all: "You will grieve, but your grief will become joy" (John 16:20).

So must we prepare our kids for life. We will not always be with them, but our modeling of trust in God, our faithfulness to our own truth, and the time we invest in guiding them to know their truth will give them the most solid foundation possible to flow with life's vicissitudes.

A woman I had on retreat, Alicia, shared this story about how she wishes she could have dealt with a major change in her life:

When I was in eighth grade, my parents bought a house in a different neighborhood, which meant I had to enroll in a new school. It was a very difficult move for me. I was quite shy and very unsure of myself in this new situation. I missed my best friend and the familiarity of classmates I had grown up with who had become almost like brothers and sisters to me. Now I was in a school community where they had all grown up together, where all the girls were expected to choose a boy they liked—but some of the girls told me the boys didn't like me. I couldn't figure out how to fit in. Overwhelmed, I retreated at first. Later, when I found my group of friends, they told me they had originally thought I was a snob. Maybe it's never easy to move at that age. Maybe adolescence is synonymous with shaky self-esteem, but I came to some realizations as the year went on. The most important was that I was likable. In reality, I didn't have to fit into anyone else's schema. I just needed to be myself. When I figured that out, I made friends. Many years later when I was teaching high school in a town with a military base, I asked a young woman named Laurel if she didn't find moving painful. "Not really," she said nonchalantly.

"There are nice people everywhere. It's just a matter of time before I meet them."

Even if our teens seem resilient, it is a mistake to think they don't need our support during times of transition. While Laurel's message, for example, may be obvious to an adult, a young person would benefit from hearing their parents speak those words. Having moved all her life, Laurel apparently learned this truth early on so that moving wasn't traumatic for her by the time she was a teenager. Alicia, on the other hand, was not prepared for the pain she experienced when change occurred. There is nothing wrong with learning the lessons of suffering. We're not helping our kids discern to protect them from heartache; rather, we're trying to provide them with tools to see greater good in the suffering that change might bring them.

Molly, age fifteen, was devastated when she learned that her friend Jamie had cancer. The next four months would change not only the summer activities they had planned together but also the fabric of their friendship. Because Molly had never experienced such a dramatic turn of events, her parents provided stability and guidance as she examined her feelings and figured out how to be a friend to Jamie in this new situation. But soon Molly launched out on her own, led by God's wisdom within her.

I didn't know what to say to Jamie at first. I finally realized that she wasn't my "sick friend"; she was my friend. I also stopped being bummed that all our summer plans were ruined. Our summer plans were just going to be different, that's all. The changes that Jamie's cancer brought weren't as bad as I thought they would be, once I accepted them. Our friendship is so much deeper now because we've shared the experience of her illness. That's a good change.

Discernment is the practice of staying in tune with God's direction within. The strength of that inner guidance has the power to transform our teens' suffering into growth.

MIDLIFE AND FAMILY CHANGE

Midlife issues effect change in the family. During their midlife years, many adults begin to question the way they've operated to this point. They realize they may not achieve their dream. They may look with fear at the ticking biological clock that will soon define their activities. They may feel panic that they've chosen the wrong career, wrong lifestyle, wrong circle of friends, wrong husband or wife, wrong just-about-everything. While adults manifest varying degrees of midlife turmoil, the change ripples throughout the entire family.

Josh remembers that time of disorder in his family. He thanks his mother for her lessons in discernment that helped him weather the turbulence:

I noticed the change in Dad when I was eleven. Sometimes I thought he didn't like me because he yelled so much, which he didn't do before. I didn't know anything about midlife crisis, so I took it personally. I do remember him talking to Mom for hours about his horrible job and his equally awful business partner, but I couldn't give sympathy for something I didn't understand. I just wanted him to play around with me like he did before.

I took on his dark moods, but my mom really worked with me through those years. She showed me how I was letting Dad define who I was, rather than defining that myself. She talked a lot about truth and God and stuff, and sometimes I thought, "Oh, that's Mom and her God-talk again," but her lessons stuck with me. I'm nineteen and starting my second year of college now, and I know who I am. I don't like that feeling of letting other people make me feel a certain way. I make my own decisions—about who I am and about what I do.

Oh, and by the way, my Dad is happy again. He's a good guy. But that still doesn't change anything about me. I am who I am.

Yes, suffering is optional in the face of change. I'm reminded of the river-rafting trips I've taken through the beautiful Glenwood Canyon in Colorado. Before we embark, the guide provides a stern lecture on safety, quizzing us on whether we know the greatest cause of drowning while rafting. Most respond that hitting one's head on a rock is probably it. "No," she says. "It's trying to resist the current. The tendency when you fall off the raft will be to try to stand upright. But don't do it. This is how people drown, because their foot gets stuck between rocks, and they're trapped. Instead, sit like you're on a chair, with your feet extended in front, and let the current carry you." In other words, go with the flow. In his book *Finding God in Troubled Times: The Holy Spirit and Suffering* (New York: Paulist Press, 1994), Richard J. Hauser, SJ, shares his awareness of "how much *additional* emotional pain we cause ourselves by our inability to face squarely and deal with the reality of our lives" (p. 5).

Sirach presents us with an option: We can choose life or death; whichever one we choose, that's what we'll get (15:17). In all life circumstances, we want our kids to be conscious that they have a choice: to move with the current or get trapped in it, to be a victor or a victim, to live fully or perish. We want them to choose life.

Chapter 11

FINE-TUNING DISCERNMENT

A COLLEAGUE in spiritual direction, also a mother, called in a panic one September evening. "Everything I've ever known about discernment has fallen apart," Kate moaned. "Can you help me sort through my emotions?"

I leaned back in my chair and put the footrest up, the phone hugging my ear. The story that unfolded was complex on several levels: the issue itself, the timing, and the fact that Kate was co-discerning with her nineteen-year-old son, who was very vulnerable at the time. As a seasoned parent, I can attest to the truth that nothing can rip a parent's heart out faster than a child in need. Even for a spiritual director, who guides dozens in discerning their path, nothing can rattle the rules of discernment more than a young person's pain. But since it wasn't my child, I had a smidgen of objectivity to offer Kate.

"As you know, Luke left for California last week to start flight school. He's wanted to be a pilot since he was five years old, or at least that's what he tells me. Truthfully, he's had so many interests and so many different goals for his life that the pilot thing didn't exactly stand out in my mind. But whatever. He's there now, after working hard toward that goal for the past two years, getting his pilot's license and putting in all those flight hours. He even threw a going-away party before he left.

"Well, two nights ago he called sounding really upset. This is what he said, as closely as I can remember it:

I think I might have made a big mistake, Mom. I just can't seem to get into it. I go to my classes and try to be interested, but I'm not. I'm not excited anymore. What's happening? I feel like I'm having a nervous breakdown or something.

Being a pilot was my dream. I told everyone I was going to do this. But when I think about the future, I don't want to live the pilot's lifestyle. I really don't. I just spent a year as a flight attendant, and it's lonely. There's no group of people to have fun with. You work with them once and either never see them again or don't remember their names next time you see them.

I don't like being away from my family and friends for days at a time, and that's what I'd be doing as a pilot. I want a job where I feel like I belong. My problem is I took out that loan, and I could get the money back if I left now. But if I wait and finish the program and then decide, I lose a lot of money. The other problem is that I told everyone I was doing this. I'm afraid I'll look like a failure if I quit now.

What's going on? I know part of it is the hijackings on September 11. That definitely spooked me. But I don't think that's what changed my mind. I can't be sure yet, but I really don't think it is. I also know part of it is that I miss Mandy. But I don't think I'm letting my girlfriend influence me. I just wish I had more time to decide. I have to decide one way or the other pretty quickly. All I want to do is get in my car and come back home.

I've talked to everyone I can think of: you, Dad, my flight instructor, my roommate, my best friends. My roommate doesn't have any of the doubts I have. But basically they all say the same thing: It's your decision.

Admittedly, Kate was caught up in her son's emotions, which fed her own. "I'm scared after the 9/11 attacks, too," she said. "Everything in me wants to tell Luke to pack his bags and come home. I feel stuck. I want to tell him to give his decision time, to get some perspective.

But he doesn't have time. He was wise to get different people's points of view, and he also showed he was trying to discern by recognizing at least two factors—the terrorist attacks and homesickness for his girlfriend—that might be clouding his judgment. He spent time reflecting on those, and was as certain as he could be that they weren't the biggest factors. I could hear his concern that people would be disappointed in him if he left, as well as disappointment in himself for backing out of a commitment. The biggest mystery for me is that he was so sure he wanted to be a pilot, and so sure—now—that he doesn't. What exactly is his longing? Which of the two is coming from his truth, authored by God?"

TAKING DISCERNMENT TO A NEW LEVEL

One of the surprises of discernment is that sincere believers often find themselves discerning between two or more positives. We get lots of practice throughout our life discerning between something good and something bad. But when both choices seem good, we take discernment to a new level, where we learn to fine-tune the process.

Sometimes the decision is such that it's impossible to tune in to a deep longing that would indicate God's direction. At other times, we need to make a decision, yet neither option thrills us. At still another time, the feeling of peace eludes us in a decision, or clarity is still murky, yet something tells us to move ahead. In cases such as these, discernment poses challenges, and we may need guidance.

Kate and I spent a long time on the phone that evening. We both discerned that Luke's *external* objections to changing his plans (the opinions of others) were overpowering his internal, growing conviction that he didn't really want to travel for his life's work.

We also discerned from what Luke said that his deepest desire *at this particular time* was to terminate pilot school and give this important, and expensive, career decision more time. Leaving was not necessarily a permanent decision; he could re-enroll at a different time. But staying was a financial investment that he may never be able to recoup.

Furthermore, we could see that Luke was actually choosing between two good choices. Being a pilot and not being a pilot are both good decisions. This may have been what was making the decision so hard for Luke.

Experience tells us that our truth can be present, but buried under a plethora of factors. For example, we've caught other people's excitement and added it to our own. We didn't recognize the "should" behind our decision. We thought of nine reasons in favor of our choice, but couldn't see the magnitude of the significant one reason that was trying to inform us otherwise. Then something of enormity happens—such as the attacks of September 11, 2001—and our truth makes itself known in a bold, unexpected way. Yes, twists are part of the spiritual journey.

Finally, we could hear in Luke's voice that he already knew his answer; he simply needed affirmation of his decision. We weren't wrong about that. Kate called again the next day. "Luke's on his way home! After agonizing for days, he said he finally reached a point where he knew he needed to leave and give the decision more time. He says he's not sure this is the right decision, but *for now* it's the best decision he can make. That was good enough for me."

Countless examples of murkiness surrounding discernment race through my head. The man who came to me four years ago feeling daily dread toward his job, yet, oddly, not feeling the desire to leave. The woman who struggled with what to do about a committed relationship that was more life-draining than life-giving. The high school senior who moved forward with a college decision, even though his two other options were equally appealing for different reasons.

Fine-tuning discernment may mean moving away from the paradigm that previously fit more clear decisions. When such questions as "What do I really want?" or "Which choice gives me peace?" don't have answers, other questions may bring more clarity.

For example:

- In imaging myself in each situation, how does it feel?
- Why has this particular decision presented itself?
- If I were counseling someone else, what would I say?
- What growth might I experience in each choice?
- What would more likely give me wholeness?
- Which of these choices best matches my gifts?
- What better helps me to reach my goal?
- Which choice is more life-giving?
- What is the loving thing to do?
- If I had three years [or one year or one month] to live, which choice would I make?
- What would Jesus do?

To take the process deeper, consider these reflection questions:

- What is my history of good discernment? When did I face a similar challenge? How did I make my decision?

- What patterns have I noticed about my longings, about what gives me life or drains me of life, and about how I love and receive love well? (Based on Dennis Linn, Sheila Fabricant Linn, and Matthew Linn, *Healing the Purpose of Your Life* [Mahwah, NJ: Paulist Press, 1999], pp. 21–22)
- What is it I *have* to do, that I can't not do? (P. 22)
- What does my body tell me about this decision? Do I feel lifted, relieved, warm inside? Or do I feel burdened, tight, or dark? What does my gut tell me?
- Am I being truly called to change, or is this internal churning part of a process that will resolve itself in time?
- If my desires are conflicting, and both are life-giving choices, which one more authentically addresses who I want to become?

DEVELOPING A HISTORY OF DISCERNMENT

Long-term spiritual direction yields a history of discernment to which we can refer when making future decisions. A gentleman who sought spiritual guidance regarding the job he hated discovered God's providence in his decision to "stick it out—at least for now." Today he barely remembers why he was so burdened four years ago. Over that time, his prayer led him to discover his penchant for perfectionism, which he learned to overcome within the context of that job. Running from the challenge, he says, would have been missing growth that has made him freer.

A woman who struggles in her relationship mentions physical and emotional symptoms, specifically chest pains and interior darkness. Her dilemma, of course, is that she has made a commitment and, in her value system, breaking vows is a serious offense.

When she reviews her history of discernment, however, she realizes, first, that she was in a broken state of mind when she made the commitment and, second, that her lifelong pattern of falling into relationships fueled her unhealthy self-perception. She continued spiritual direction and also made the decision that *for now* she would stay in the relationship while healing with psychotherapy. But she is quick to add: "The decision isn't over yet. When I can see with clearer eyes, I'll make a decision about the relationship."

A young man reflects on his college choice, "The opportunity was so great, I couldn't *not* do it." Desiring a more diverse environment, and wanting to try out-of-state living, this was his opportunity. Furthermore, the college held a specific major that fit his gifts better than two other colleges he was considering. "It was a tough decision," he concludes, "but this school calls to me in a way the others didn't. I think I can be more myself here."

Joseph A. Tetlow, SJ, author of *Choosing Christ in the World* (Saint Louis: Institute of Jesuit Sources, 1989), says this about the role of desire—and hazy desires—in discernment:

> Our original purpose expresses itself naturally in our desiring. That is how we know what we are "supposed to do" with our lives. . . .
>
> . . . Out of my dynamic original purpose rise great desires. Out of it come what I want to do with my life and what I want to become. But I am aware of having many desires, even conflicting desires. I may be aware, for example, of truly wanting to be a priest

and also of authentically wanting to be married. I may be aware of desiring deeply to serve the poor and yet of desiring deeply to provide an altogether-adequate living for my children. If I love God steadily and without breaching our relationship all my life, then I progressively feel those desires clearly and forcibly; I know with sureness what I want to do and to become. No human being can tell me that, and no one needs to. (P. 204)

Our adolescents' fuzzy decision making tempts us to jump in and take over. But we don't need to. Instead, we help them fine-tune their discernment. The clarity they receive fosters healthier choices.

Chapter 12

DISCERNMENT AND TIME

TIME nurtures discernment. I have watched countless faith-filled people struggle with decisions, but then arrive at that moment when truth is revealed. Swirling in the darkest cycle of a decision, it seems like an answer will never come. Yet, as I accompany them on their spiritual journey, I know that resolution is likely just around the corner, echoing the adage that the sky is darkest just before dawn.

When resolution seems to evade a decision, the discerner has likely not allowed enough time for the hallmarks of a good discernment to reveal themselves. Time is always on the side of the one discerning. Those of us who have lived long enough to appreciate long-term indecision and turmoil know that the gifts of time are resolution, growth, and closure.

ALL IN GOD'S TIME

As a teenager, whenever I went shopping with my mother, her consistent response to my desire to buy something was, "Think about it for a day or two, then come back if you still want it." Frankly, her advice drove me crazy. But to this day I still use that guideline when considering purchases—because it works. Time helps sift out genuine desire from impulse.

The same is true with other decisions. Maturity brings patience, but until then, parents can guide kids to be patient with the process of discernment. By sharing our own experiences of God's faithfulness, for example, we help our emerging young adults know they can count on God to reveal divine will—in time. Decision by decision, we help kids develop a history of God's answers to their prayer and of the amount of time it took to hear God's voice.

A visiting preacher once delighted the congregation with his homily about God's sometimes agonizingly slow response. He alluded to the Woody Allen movie *Love and Death* (1975), in which Allen's character, Boris, is executed in front of a firing squad, despite having had a vision that he would escape this fate. The camera zooms in on postmortem Boris as he speaks: "If it turns out there is a God, I don't think he's evil. I think the worst you can say about him is that basically he's an underachiever." A basic tenet of discernment: God *will* reveal God's will—in time.

TIME PROVIDES RESOLUTION

A young man named David remembers taking his first part-time job in high school and hating it. His inner feeling of distaste was worth listening to. Perhaps he had chosen the wrong place to work. On the other hand, his negative feeling was not in itself an indication that he should quit his job. David's parents suggested that he give it time, explaining that one of their family's values was a work ethic of commitment. This directive made David mad. He was sure a better job was out there somewhere. Besides, his friends weren't forced to stay in jobs they didn't like.

After several months, though, David gradually grew to like his place of employment. In fact, it became the heart of his social group throughout high school and college, something he never would have predicted based on his initial feelings. David was able to see how a rough start resolved itself over time, a powerful lesson for future decisions.

Some experiences are painful, but necessary for growth. With such events, time is the lens that can perceive the wisdom of our discernment. Sue recalled a period of struggle in her career:

I changed careers after twelve years in the same position. The yearning to be a high school counselor was so strong I couldn't ignore it. So I enrolled at the university, got a counseling degree, and went to work in a high school. I was so sure I would love this job that I even bought a house near the school.

Before the year was out, though, I was miserable. The politics at the school made life unbearable. The chairman of the counseling department was, at best, insensitive and rude; at worst, she was downright cruel to me. Everyone I talked to—family, friends, counselors—advised me to get out of that toxic environment. I prayed fiercely about this situation. After a time, I took the steps necessary to be considered for other positions in the district—so I wouldn't feel so trapped. But something deep inside was not allowing me to quit. Was it pride? Lack of courage? A perverse desire to punish myself? I prayed about all these possibilities.

As time went on, I came to a powerful realization: I needed to learn how to deal with conflict. If I didn't do it here at this job, I would face the same issues elsewhere. That insight transformed me. I knew, at last, that there was divine purpose to my being in this place at this time. I suffered for three years at that school, often feeling hopeless, but by giving it time I was able to arrive at a point where I could hear God's wisdom. I made the decision not to be a victim any longer. I learned some peacemaking and assertiveness skills and began using them. I think I have a lot to share with the students I counsel as a result of this experience: Give your decisions time.

However, sometimes the feelings of aversion are a sign that change is in order. As always, time will allow God's direction to be known. Sixteen-year-old Caitlin found herself in a situation that made her feel uneasy and with time she learned the value of listening to the voice of wisdom within:

When I started my new job, the assistant manager, Bob, gave the orientation for new employees. He was okay, I guess, but something about him made me feel funny. One of my friends once told me that I come down hard on people, like I'm judgmental, so I've been trying to give people the benefit of the doubt. I figured I was being judgmental again with Bob, so I guess you could say I decided to keep an open mind.

When I told my dad that Bob was pretty nice, but kind of creepy, he told me to trust my feelings and just keep my eyes open. Funny thing, my dad came into the store the next day and asked Bob about a product. I thought, hmm . . .

Actually, Bob was really friendly to me. He was fun to talk to, and we laughed a lot together, and he always complimented me on my work. I got to thinking I had made a mistake about him. Now he didn't seem creepy at all. I thought maybe this was one of those lessons about loving one another and getting to know people in order to discover their goodness. My mom is a big one for that.

Still, after I had been working for about a month, I noticed Bob staring at me when he thought I wasn't looking. When he kept doing it, it kind of freaked me. The other thing I noticed is that Bob scheduled me to work every time he was working. When he was off, I was off. When he was on, I was on. One time, he was reading an inventory form over my shoulder. He didn't exactly do anything, but it just seemed like he was way too close. I didn't like it. But I told myself I was getting paranoid.

One night my dad asked me about Bob. He wanted to know if I was still feeling funny about him. I told him everything I had been feeling, and he said just one word: "Quit."

I never felt so relieved in my life. I don't know if Bob was dangerous to me or not because I didn't hang around long enough to find out. But I'm glad my dad freed me to trust my feelings.

RELATIONSHIPS AND CLOSURE

A long discernment can reap the gift of closure. Young love holds bountiful examples. Time reveals whether a relationship is life-giving or not, what incompatibilities exist, what gold is buried within the other. If a relationship appears to have run its course, time has the power to give the young person the conviction and the courage to break it off. Nineteen-year-old Roberto is learning to value time in his current relationship:

Ashley and I have been dating for three years. I like everything about her. But last summer I started having this feeling inside that something's not right. That's the best way I can describe it. I guess we have different goals for our lives that don't seem to fit. It's funny how everything was great for two-and-a-half years, then all of a sudden it wasn't.

I still like Ashley. Sometimes I feel like we could date forever because we get along so well. We're still together. It doesn't feel like time to break up yet. I'm going to give it time before I say anything to Ashley because I want to be sure. But I'm 99 percent positive we're not meant to be lifetime partners.

Jill is grateful her parents were there to guide her when she became engaged at eighteen:

John asked me to marry him the month before he was leaving for the Marines. He told me he wanted someone to come home to. I was ecstatic. We had been together for two years, so I felt like I knew him well. But my parents had other ideas. I could see by their reaction that they were concerned. They didn't forbid me from marrying him, or even from becoming engaged. Good thing, because if they had, I would have sided with John, and probably married him right away. What I agreed to was to wait at least a year and a half.

That next year was an eye opener for me. I started realizing how possessive John was. He didn't want me to even go out with my friends while he was gone. What was I supposed to do for the next year and a half? It was crazy. Over the next few months, I learned he had plenty of plans for what I should do with my life without any regard for my dreams. By the time he came home for his first long leave, I was in turmoil. Part of me was thrilled to be with him again, but an even bigger part of me quivered inside. Fortunately, my parents had raised me to listen to my intuition. Told me it was a gift from God. I never felt so free as I did when I broke off my engagement to John. Good thing I gave it time.

Time also brings healing and clear vision to the one who is hurting. Sixteen-year-old Dani was shattered when she found out her boyfriend was gravitating to her best friend. When Jeremy finally called Dani to break up with her, she was devastated. Her whole demeanor changed. This once sunny, outgoing young woman who walked confidently into the house each day took on a somber, melancholy disposition that lasted for nearly a year.

Her mother was saddened, too, as mothers can be. What she really wanted to do was hang Jeremy up by his toes, but instead Michelle wisely let Dani heal in her own way at her own pace. She assured her daughter that this kind of pain was not God's will, that God was most likely crying right along with her, and that with time she would get a clearer picture of the situation.

Dani can look back now without pain or anger and thank God she's no longer with Jeremy. She says her discernment has given her insights that will help her in her next relationship. "It was kind of like my pain just gradually diminished till finally it wasn't there anymore," Dani says now. "I have new life." But it took time. As for Michelle, she admits sheepishly, "Dani closed this chapter a lot faster than I did." But she never told her daughter that.

Time is always on the side of the discerner. Jesus told a parable comparing the Reign of God to the person who sowed good seed in the field (Matt. 13:24–30). Unfortunately, enemies came and planted weeds among the wheat, and the weeds made their appearance as the wheat crop began to mature and yield grain. Rather than pulling the weeds and possibly taking the wheat with it, the farmer decided to let them grow together until harvest. At that point, he would yank the weeds and burn them, then gather the wheat. Giving the crop time yields clarity to distinguish between weeds and wheat. Discernment allows healthy choices to take root and grow into maturity, keeping the weeds at bay. But it's a process. And it takes time.

Chapter 13

WHEN A TEENAGER NEEDS MORE EXTERNAL CONTROL

BEING a "good Christian family" holds no guarantee that our families will waltz through life problem free. We are part of the human condition. Even kids who have been raised to be discerning need external control at times. Katie, for example, was fourteen when she stopped doing homework. Her concerned teachers and frantic parents were unable to come up with a plan to motivate her to succeed. Katie simply didn't want to do her schoolwork.

Seventeen-year-old Thomas felt perfectly innocent in his role as lookout for his companions while they pilfered beer after hours from the back room of the store where they worked. After all, he didn't steal anything. His employer thought otherwise; he lost his job.

Mark was an impulsive child from the time he first hoisted himself onto his feet. He ran his parents ragged with his hyperactivity, frazzled his teachers with his distractibility, and peppered his life with one poor decision after another. As a ten-year-old, he broke windows at neighbors' homes simply for the sport of it. At fifteen, he was in an accident after taking his parents' car while they slept. As a nineteen-year-old, he was arrested for selling his Ritalin to coworkers.

Some children simply need more external control. No responsible parent would encourage Katie's desire to avoid schoolwork. No parent intent upon instilling moral values in her or his child would leave Thomas on his own to discern his use of leisure time without some guidance. As close as Mark is to the independence of adulthood, his parents are not yet finished with their influence on him.

Clearly, parents are responsible for their children's safety and well-being. Communicating about discernment within the family does not preclude that some children at some point will need extra external control. Teens who fall in with a destructive crowd, those whose body chemistry adversely affects their behavior, students who stop working in school, and young people with addictions need direct guidelines about what decisions are acceptable. When these situations occur, parents must tighten the reins on their adolescent's activities, voice their concerns that their teen's choices are not life-giving, and work closely to rebuild the discernment paradigm.

Keep in mind that empowering a child to discern is a process, one that begins, ideally, at a very young age. For some young people, learning to discern will be a longer process, which may be interrupted with periods when parents temporarily take control of their children's choices, all the while talking through the rationale of each decision. The goal is to gradually release responsibility for decision making to the children as they grow in responsibility, maturity, and spiritual insight.

Parents need to use their own gift of discernment. When an adolescent shows a pattern of poor decisions, parents must follow up on any interior disquiet they experience surrounding that child. Many times the young person has taken pains to hide visible clues of her or his poor choices. Parents then need to rely on and trust their intuition, which is a gift from God to be honored.

HANNAH'S JOURNEY

Kunal and Karen were devastated when they realized that their daughter, Hannah, was living a double life right before their eyes:

Hannah shocked us when she told us she wanted to attend Alcoholics Anonymous. We were completely caught off guard. We loved her friends and always knew where she was. But what we didn't know—and what she spelled out to us as we listened, horrified—was that she had begun drinking, just a little bit, a year and a half before and had since slid—sip by sip—into a full-fledged addiction. We had always trusted her to make good decisions, but in that one moment of exposure, all that changed. For now, we were going to make the decisions.

The next two years were a nightmare. To make a long, arduous story short, we restructured her life into a box a fraction of the size she had been used to. It was June, so she had plenty of time to attend AA meetings. We also got her into counseling. Her only other allowed activity was her job. If not at one of those three places, she was at home. The toughest decision we made was to pull her out of her high school and enroll her in another that was twenty-five miles away, near Kunal's work. We knew how hard it would be for her to break away from her old group and find acceptance among the kind of kids who could help her along if she stayed at the same school. We felt she needed a clean slate.

But Hannah was mad. Boy, was she mad. She thought it was enough that she had taken the initiative to get sober. She didn't want all those other infringements on her freedom. This normally agreeable young woman was now miserable to be around. She resented us and took every opportunity to let us know that. I think she was really scared, but it came across as anger. And we took the brunt of it.

We know a lot of kids would have rebelled even more at such restriction, sneaking out, maybe even running away, and so perhaps we were lucky. But I think deep inside Hannah was relieved that we had stepped in and taken over the decision making that had become too hard for her. It was her idea, after all, to find healing for her addiction. She cried and cried when we told her she would be going to a new school—that was the worst part for her—and that made it hard for us, too. Who was to say she might not attract the same crowd she had at her first school? There were so many uncertainties. But we knew we had to trust our best judgment, and we trusted that God was leading. We were about as vulnerable as two people could be, so trust was all we could depend on.

Once parents discern that significant growth has taken place, they encourage the child to once again trust God's movement within. This is a gradual, prayerful process, but a necessary one. In this process parents walk side by side with the child, as closely as they did when they were first teaching him or her to discern. They are, in effect, starting over. Hannah's parents concluded:

We have to admit it was scary letting Hannah make her own decisions. We waited till she had been sober a year. That meant that her entire junior year, she did only what we allowed her to do. We constantly monitored her activities and, yes, her phone calls and e-mails. As she began her senior year, we continued to monitor her activities, but we stayed more in the background. Our eyes were wide open, but we encouraged her to make the decisions. We reminded Hannah of her goodness, complimented her on her mature decision to get help when her life was out of control, talked through her choices with her, helped her recognize the feelings of peace and certitude when she made a good decision, affirmed her endlessly.

As the year went on, we slowly placed decisions in her hands and kept our input to a minimum. It was so hard letting go, but we knew that if we didn't bring her to a point where she could make healthy choices for herself, her life after graduation could be tumultuous. One of our relatives was quite vocal about how we were setting Hannah free too soon. That may be true for some kids. But Kunal and I were extremely careful about staying in tune with Hannah, and, believe me, we prayed for wisdom with more fervor than we ever thought we had. We felt strong about the steps we had taken and the timetable we followed. We, too, had to stay true to what we discerned to be God's voice in our decisions.

The road of life can be a bumpy one. When we encounter challenging situations such as what Hannah's family faced, it is understandable that our faith in the discernment process can begin to shake, if not crumble. But as much as we wish otherwise, God never promised to spare us from the human condition. Yet, God does promise to be with us through it all. Sometimes that hope is all that holds us together. Life provides countless opportunities to live in faith. Indeed, the unknown pervades our existence. But our help is God's Spirit, filling us with the wisdom to discern what will give our families life. Our response is to accept the gift of discernment graciously. And use it.

Chapter 14

MISTAKES IN DISCERNMENT

WHAT IF we spend years fostering discernment in our youth, only to watch them make foolish choices? What about the big issues I hear parents bemoaning to their water aerobics partners and anyone else who will listen: parting from our faith tradition to explore another (or to explore nothing), marrying someone who we can see is not good for them, living with a boyfriend or girlfriend outside of marriage, having an abortion, making risky financial investments, dropping out of school, entering into a career that doesn't seem to use their gifts?

FAMILY DIFFERENCES

It would be a mistake to expect that nourishing the gift of discernment in our families will necessarily result in perfect harmony of values, visions, and goals among family members. In fact, if we truly value the fruit of discernment, namely that each family member is free to be her or his truest self, then we can surely expect diversity. Still, when our children's values directly oppose what we have always cherished, we become sad and concerned.

Carolyn called her sister one day seeking advice: "What do I tell Dominic about Tanya? They're talking about getting engaged. But she's awful for him. I'm afraid if I say something, he'll dig his heels in further. I've worked with him on making good choices for so many years that I just don't understand how he decided on her. Am I being overprotective of my firstborn? Am I too picky? I think he's making a big mistake."

Carolyn must discern a way to solve her dilemma before she can effectively co-discern with her son. Furthermore, when to speak, what to say, and if to speak at all are questions parents must entrust to the Holy Spirit. God will guide the co-discerning parent.

On Dominic's part, the choice of a life partner is, of course, his own. If we were to poll the world, we would find countless examples of marriages that flourished despite family protests, and countless others that failed despite family approval. Carolyn can trust that Dominic's discernment is where God will meet him, and that he will learn to grow through his decisions. Nevertheless, as a co-discerner, she will share insights with Dominic as she can best discern from God's voice within.

Peter and Christina, parents of three, will never forget the day their son Anthony dropped a bomb on them:

We were so stunned when Anthony announced that he and Hong were planning a commitment ceremony. We feel naive that we missed it, but we really had no clue he was gay. Our first thought was that we had failed as parents. Our second worry was that he was not acceptable in the eyes of the Church and of God. Our third concern was how we were going to keep this from friends and family. This news just about knocked us out. It was a time of huge turmoil.

We felt so out of control, all we could do was pray. We didn't know it at the time, but we were in for a few surprises. Through God's wisdom, we were led to research homosexuality, from both a psychological viewpoint and a spiritual perspective. We read both sides of the issue, talked with other parents of homosexuals, spent hours with Anthony and his partner trying to understand what it was like for them, and, of course, we prayed. As we shared with each other, we soon found ourselves in a place of peace, hard to verbalize, but which continued to deepen. Hong and Anthony are living their truth. They didn't create their orientation; it's who they are. We can't know firsthand what Anthony and Hong's love means, but we do know we love them with all our hearts. They can count on that. And if we love them so deeply, how much more must God love them?

Sadly, not all stories turn out so well. Homosexuality splits apart families on a regular basis. But God's law is a law of love, and families I've talked to who sincerely seek God's wisdom report that the acceptance they come to through prayer surpasses all understanding. As Peter said, "I know with certitude that God asks me to have the same unconditional love for my children that God has for me."

REJECTING RELIGION

When kids tell us they don't want to share our religious affiliation, that what we had taught them no longer makes sense, we can feel unnerved. Howard, fervent in his faith, felt defeated when each one of his four children left the faith he had raised them in:

I don't get it. I thought I was doing a good job modeling the faith for them. Weekly worship was a given in our family. All the kids went to parochial schools. What did I do wrong?

Having shared spiritual conversations with hundreds, I know that we are each on our own unique journey, guided by God, who is ever vigilant. I have spoken with numerous women and men who have questioned their faith, some who have even questioned the existence of God. Of all the stories I've heard, most people arrive at a deeper faith *because* they took the time to examine what they had learned. Some choose to remain affiliated with their church; others leave. Still others align themselves with a different denomination that feeds them in a way that is authentic for them. But none remain estranged from God for very long. As Saint Augustine admitted in his *Confessions*, "You have made us for yourself, Lord, and our hearts are restless until they rest in you" (Frank Sheed, trans., *The Confessions of St. Augustine* [New York: Sheed and Ward, 1943], p. 1, as quoted in Ronald Rolheiser, *The Holy Longing: The Search for a Christian Spirituality* [New York: Doubleday, 1999], p. 5). Perhaps the appropriate prayer for our children is that they will stay true to their journey toward union with God, wherever that path leads them.

WAS IT A MISTAKE?

The fact that a situation turns out badly, that obstacles keep appearing, or that trials are built into the new choice is not in itself a signpost of a poor discernment.

Eighteen-year-old Angie saved long and hard to buy her first car. She took her time, reading consumer reports on the Internet, comparing prices through the newspaper, looking at various used cars at dealerships, listening to the advice of her parents and other knowledgeable adults. When she had gathered enough funds, Angie set out to make her purchase. She located a car that felt right, then went home and gave it time. The next day, she bought the perfect car. But the car proved to be a lemon. After six months, and more repairs than she had ever bargained for, Angie sold her car.

Did Angie discern wrongly? Key to discernment is this tenet: The result of the discernment is not the determining factor in a good discernment. Life is too variable, the human condition too capricious, to assure that any outcome of a decision will necessarily be favorable. Instead, the focus is on the *process* of discernment. When young people use the tools of discernment, as Angie did, then come to a place of peace, we can support them in their decisions and encourage them to move forward.

When a decision has an undesirable outcome, the only purpose for looking back is to review the process to see if it broke down at some point. Agonizing over the result of a decision made in faith bears no fruit.

Jared chose to attend college where most of his friends were going, but he wasn't simply following the crowd. No, he decided, this feels right, and his parents concurred. During that first year, though, Jared tuned in to another longing that became stronger as the year went on. Finally, he shared with his parents that he believed art school would feed his passion. After visiting two schools, he decided to enroll in the commercial art program offered at a nearby trade school.

Was Jared's year in college a false start—a mistake? Not by any means. He is the first to acknowledge that no one can take away the learning he accomplished that year, nor the gaggle of friends he made, some of them lifelong. Many adults know the same experience of ongoing discernment, considering that most adults change careers several times in their lifetime.

DISCERNMENT DOES NOT PROTECT FROM HARDSHIP

The spiritual road is not without bumps, ruts, and detours. Life will try us, but ours is an optimistic faith. We have the promise that God is with us always (Matt. 28:20), that death has no power (2 Tim. 1:10), that we can pass through raging waters without drowning (Isa. 43:2), that all things are possible (Mark 10:27), that Jesus came so we might have life in abundance (John 10:10), that grace is more powerful than sin (2 Cor. 12:9), that God always forgives (Col. 3:13), that the Kingdom is here and now (Matt. 4:17), and that God dwells within (John 14:17), closer to us than we are to ourselves.

Like our God who never abandons us, healthy families support one another, even when a decision seemingly backfires. When a discernment results in pain for our teenagers, we stand by them, encouraging them to tune in to God, listen, and act in accordance with what they discern to be God's guidance. If they look back, it is only to examine their faithfulness to the process of discernment, not to accuse themselves of poor discerning. Feeling pain in the wake of a decision can be most unsettling for emerging young adults, whose history of trusting God is still new. Now more than ever they need us to model the gentle compassion of God and reassure them that God is with them as they move forward.

When we fear our adolescent has erred, or when we see distress as he or she re-examines the process that led to pain in his or her choice, our faith in discernment can be challenged. We take our responsibility as parents seriously, in fact making a lifetime career of it, but ultimately our children are in God's transforming embrace. The following prayer may help us trust God's providence in discernment:

Letting Go
Author unknown

To a dear one about whom I have been concerned.

I behold the Christ in you.
I place you lovingly in the care of the Father.

I release you from my anxiety and concern.
I let go of my possessive hold on you.
I am willing to free you to follow the dictates of your
indwelling Lord.
I am willing to free you to live your life according to
your best light and understanding.
Husband, wife, child, friend—
I no longer try to force my ideas on you, my ways on
you.
I lift my thoughts above you, above the personal
level.
I see you as God sees you, a spiritual being, created
in His image, and endowed with qualities
and abilities that make you needed, and
important—not only to me but to God and
His larger plan.
I do not bind you. I no longer believe that you do
not have the understanding you need in
order to meet life.
I bless you,
    I have faith in you,
        I behold Jesus in you.

(From John Veltri, SJ, *A Collection of Helps for Prayer,* vol. 1 of
Orientations [Guelph, Ontario: Loyola House, 1979], p. 100)

Chapter 15

DISCERNMENT AND FAMILY WELL-BEING

AS WE CLOSE, it's time to dream. While we accept that our family is perfectly imperfect, we move toward fostering a home environment we've always dreamed of: where kids want to spend time, where they feel proud to bring their friends, where adult children return. It's a home where kids can be themselves, and family members breathe easy, free of expectations they can't possibly meet. Parents and children alike feel good about themselves. Laughter flows thick and rich from souls who feel safe, supported, assured.

Believe it or not, these scenarios are not limited to Hallmark, Norman Rockwell, or Grandma Moses. The fruits of discernment are myriad, and ultimately they contribute to the wellness of the family. Family well-being and family spirituality go hand in hand. When family members spend time together, build healthy relationships with one another, and solve conflicts and reconcile with one another, they grow not only in wholeness but also in faith.

As families center themselves in God and nourish their gift of discernment, they can look forward to these benefits:

- Openness and transparency
- Good communication
- Bonding of the deepest nature with the superglue of faith
- A sense of well-being
- Confidence rather than fear or insecurity
- Freedom for parents and children

- Wholeness
- Mutual respect in the family
- Acceptance of differences
- Harmony within self and among family members
- Healthy relationships within and outside the family
- Tools for solving conflicts and reconciliation
- Opportunities to live faith in the concrete
- An atmosphere of support for making thoughtful, mature decisions
- Deep faith based on a healthy image of God
- Peace
- Love
- Joy

PARENTAL DISAGREEMENT

When I talk about discernment on retreats, a question often arises: "I'm trying to empower our teens to make decisions that are true and right for them, but my spouse insists on making decisions for them. Despite our efforts to talk about it, we still have different viewpoints, and it's causing disharmony. What should I do?"

Without a clear-cut answer, I appeal to the wisdom of the group, most of them experienced parents. As expected, answers vary:

- Keep talking to your spouse about discernment.
- Get counseling.
- Give up the idea of discernment in order to present a united front for the children.
- Teach the kids to discern anyway without saying anything negative about your spouse's approach.
- Grab the kids and go hide in a cave until they're grown up.
- Pray.

Bottom line: we are each accountable to our own unique truth authored by God. The Spirit's gifts of wisdom, understanding, and knowledge are available for building this Kingdom called the family. What to say to a child, and when to say it, is often a moment-by-moment discernment. As Jesus prepared his Apostles well and entrusted them to his Holy Spirit when he left this life, we must do the same for our children. To do otherwise is to compromise our integrity before God.

RECONCILIATION

Discernment fosters reconciliation, which is crucial to family well-being. A middle-aged man named Peter, who learned of discernment on a retreat, had a poignant tale about a family that could have been:

Generally speaking, I had a good childhood, and Mom and Dad did a good job raising me and my brothers and sister. But now that we're all adults, subtle and not-so-subtle factions have seeped into the family. I realize we were not very accepting of each other.

It started with my folks. They had great expectations for all of us. Yeah, I know they thought they were preparing us for the best life possible. But my sister entered the field they wanted for her because she believed that because our parents pushed her in that direction, it must be right for her. She just about withered and died in that career; it didn't match her gifts at all.

People couldn't just be people. I heard a lot of criticism of neighbors and relatives, and I remember thinking that I never wanted to be criticized like that. So I was careful to be as perfect as possible, always anticipating how my actions or words might be perceived. Believe me, that's a stressful way to live, and it wasn't necessary. It took me years to learn that those potential critics I was so afraid of either didn't exist or had issues of their own that made them find flaws in me.

Then there was the fighting. Sure, siblings fight. But we put each other down. We didn't have any appreciation for differences. Wouldn't it have been just as easy to help us see that our differences were valuable as it was to tell us to stop fighting? I'm sounding harsh, and I don't want to. It's just that there really was another way.

I'm no saint either. I made fun of some of my kid brother's choices. That wasn't right. He was doing what was right for him. How can I expect us to be open with each other when everyone's afraid of being judged?

What I've learned from praying with discernment is the power of forgiveness. I got married before I was mature enough to make such a commitment. When I got divorced, one of my brothers told me how wrong I was, then distanced himself from me after that. That stung. At first I was mad, but deep down I figured he thought I was unworthy of him. I've carried resentment toward him for more years than I can count. I've been thinking a lot about two things. For one, when my marriage ended I did the only thing I could have done at the time. It was horrible for both of us. Even though I didn't know about discernment, I didn't make the decision without thought. So I should forgive myself.

And the second thing is, I have to let my brother be who he is. He has a good heart in a lot of ways. If he's misguided in rebuking me, that's between God and him. For my own mental health, though, I think I can try to see him for who he is and let my resentment go. I have a new resolve to reconcile with my family. Even though I never overtly expressed hostility toward them, I know I'll approach them with a much more open and peaceful heart. That's healthier for me for sure. But it's healthy for our family, too.

My kids are teenagers now. I'm going to start talking to them about discernment. I want them to make career choices that are their own and to feel good about it. I want them to honor each other, even when they differ in opinions or preferences. I want harmony in our family. I just hope it's not too late.

It's not too late. The gifts of the Holy Spirit are ours to use in building strong, loving, spiritually mature families. The Hallmark kind, but with splotches of reality.

The dream is not over. It's only beginning, because it doesn't stop with our generation. We are using the gifts God gave us for God's purpose: to build the Kingdom. As our children help their children discern, families are healthier, the Church is stronger, the Kingdom is transformed. We can internalize what Moses proposed to the Israelites: He set before them life and death and implored them to choose life so that they and their descendants might live a long life, by loving God, heeding God's voice, and holding fast to God (Deut. 30:19–20). Choose life. It's a healthy choice.

QUESTIONS FOR REFLECTION AND SHARING

The following questions are for personal reflection and for sharing between couples or within a study group:

CHAPTER 1: BECOMING A DISCERNING ADULT

- What does the word *charity* mean to you? What does charity look like when you're practicing or receiving it? What does it *not* look like?
- Think of a time when the Holy Spirit spoke to you in a powerful and personal way. What vessels did the Spirit use?
- Do you trust your longings? If not, what prevents you from trusting? If so, what experiences confirm that your longings are authored by God?
- What does a disquieting inner voice sound like to you? What is your experience of heeding this voice?
- What is your experience of prayer?

CHAPTER 2: DISCERNMENT AND DEVELOPING A HEALTHY IMAGE OF GOD

- When you hear, "God is love," what perceptions of love come to mind—positive or negative?
- How does it make you feel that young people come to know God through our person?
- God has many ways to reveal love to our children. How have you seen this in your family?

- Who is God for you?
- How has your image of God evolved? What factors have influenced your image of God?

CHAPTER 3: QUALITIES OF A CO-DISCERNING PARENT

- How important is it to affirm your adolescent's personal integrity, that is, her or his sense of what is true and right?
- Are you prayerful? If so, what does that look like? If not, what barriers keep you from being open to prayer?
- Have you manifested humility in an authentic way, according to its rightful meaning?
- Do you trust God and your teenager? If not, where does your lack of trust originate?
- How can you make your teen feel that you're completely in love with his or her person?
- How do you listen to your adolescent's desires without forcing your own agenda?

CHAPTER 4: TOOLS FOR CO-DISCERNMENT

- Knowledge of self and knowledge of God go hand in hand. What does this mean to you? How have you experienced the truth of this statement?
- What are your family's values? In other words, what behaviors are non-negotiable in your family?
- Describe a decision someone in your family made that clarified the difference between the *process* of discernment and the choice itself.
- Never make decisions in periods of darkness, if possible, and never change an authentic discernment during a bleak time. Does this statement reflect your own wisdom according to your experience?
- Reflect on a time when you made the best decision you could, given the information you had, the circumstances,

and your ability to sense certitude at that particular moment. What did that experience tell you about discernment?

- In your family, how can you feasibly teach young children the principles of discernment?
- Your teen is turned off to religious talk right now. How can you help her or him discern during this time?

CHAPTER 5: CO-DISCERNING PARENTS IN ACTION

- What do you want most for your teenager?
- Children are not things to be molded, but people to be unfolded. How does this statement fit with your family and with your personal philosophy of parenting?
- Where do you see God's will fitting in with *your* will? With your teenager's will?
- What does healthy spirituality mean to you?

CHAPTER 6: DISCERNMENT AND PEER PRESSURE

- As an adult, do you ever feel peer pressure? How have you handled it?
- What wisdom would you pass on to your emerging young adult that he or she would hear and believe?
- What do you do to make your home a safe haven for kids to believe in themselves?
- When you were a teenager, did you wander from your parents' values? Why or why not?

CHAPTER 7: DISCERNMENT AND PERFECTIONISM

- How do you know when you've crossed the line between demanding perfection and empowering your teen to do her or his personal best?

- When you were a teenager, were you completely accepted by your parents for who you were? If not, how did you know you weren't? Are you completely accepted by them now? If not, how do you know you aren't?
- Do you completely accept your kids as they are? If so, how do you let them know this?
- What signs do you recognize when your adolescent is being true to the core of who he or she is? How do you know when he or she is being true to *you* instead?
- "Living the truth in love, we should grow in every way into him who is the head, Christ" (Eph. 4:15). What does this quotation mean to you?
- Think of a time when you led your teenager to believe she or he had fallen short of perfection. How might that scenario look if instead you were to help that child realize how a particular choice had impeded freedom, placed her or him in turmoil, or decreased joy?
- How can you create a tone of levity in your home so that family members don't take themselves too seriously?

CHAPTER 8: DISCERNMENT AND FRIENDSHIPS

- When have you felt a gnawing inside in the context of a relationship? What did that feeling mean for you at the time? What does that experience mean for you in retrospect?
- Where did your strong—or struggling—sense of self come from? What are you doing to foster a strong sense of self in your adolescent?
- People are different from, not better or worse than, one another. Does your family believe this? How do you know?
- What factors—internal and external—make it hard for you to pray, then sit back and let God work in your child's heart?

- How do you teach your teenager to set boundaries with friends? What roadblocks have you run into?
- When have you experienced a shift in a relationship? How did you resolve it in a way that brought you interior peace? What advice will you share with your teen when this happens to him or her?
- How can you support your adolescent who is trying to help a friend who has severe problems?

CHAPTER 9: DISCERNMENT AND SEXUALITY

- How do you experience sexuality as distinct from genitality?
- How did your impressions of sexuality evolve? Is there any area that needs healing?
- What wisdom surrounding sexuality have you shared with your children? Were they able to hear you? Why or why not?
- What wisdom surrounding sexuality will you share with your children?
- What do you remember about the sexual revolution of your youth? What did you learn from your perceptions and experiences during that time?
- Whatever our early sexual experiences, they can hold richness for our children if we pass on the insight we gained from them. If these experiences are kept in the darkness, they take on a life that fills the air with disquiet, which our teenagers sense but don't understand. Do you agree or disagree? In what way specifically?
- Would you want your teenager to hear Kevin and Courtney's story? If so, what lessons might it hold? If not, why?

CHAPTER 10: DISCERNMENT AND CHANGE

- Share your history of change and how you handled it each time. What wisdom can you share with your teen regarding change?
- Describe a specific change in the life of your family that brought your family to a new, higher level of integrity, value, and confidence in following their truth.
- How did your parents' midlife issues affect you? How might yours be affecting your children? How will this awareness impact how you relate to your teens during this time?

CHAPTER 11: FINE-TUNING DISCERNMENT

- What factors make certain decisions more difficult than others?
- In your discernment history, what processes have you used to discern difficult decisions? What has worked? What hasn't?
- In your experience, do most, some, or few of the decisions you make have a clear right or wrong answer?
- Share a decision you or a family member made for which several good options were possible. How did you or the family member know that the decision was true and right for you or for him or her?
- Share a decision that you or a family member discerned that surprised you. How do you now see God's providence at work in that decision?
- Reflect on the quotation from Joseph Tetlow (*Choosing Christ in the World*) on pages 99–100. Does it resonate with your personal history of discernment? If so, share examples.

CHAPTER 12: DISCERNMENT AND TIME

- In your discernment history, what have you learned about God's sometimes agonizingly slow response? What wisdom would you share with your child about this?
- God *will* reveal God's will—in time. Is this true in your experience?
- Sue realized there was divine purpose to her staying in a work environment that tested her patience when she received the insight that this was her opportunity to learn to deal with conflict. As you read her story, what insights did you receive?
- Share how you successfully separate yourself from your adolescent's emotional state when he or she is trying to make a decision in the midst of his or her pain. How do you help him or her make healthy decisions when he or she is in darkness?

CHAPTER 13: WHEN A TEENAGER NEEDS MORE EXTERNAL CONTROL

- Consider an experience you had when you were an adolescent in which your parents needed to tighten the reins on you. How did you feel at the time? What wisdom or lack of wisdom do you now see in how your parents handled you?
- Reflect on a time when you had to exert more external control over your teen. What did you learn about discernment from this experience?
- Share an experience that shook your faith in the discernment process. How has that experience affected your approach to discernment?

CHAPTER 14: MISTAKES IN DISCERNMENT

- What values, visions, and goals do you hold for yourself and your teen? How do you reconcile these with the value of wanting your child to be free to be her or his truest self?
- What would be the hardest thing for you to accept about your teen? Spend some time imagining what you might say to her or him if this were to happen.
- Perhaps a more appropriate prayer for our children is that they will stay true to their journey toward union with God, wherever that path leads them. Is such a general prayer easy or hard for you?
- Share an experience when it was difficult for you to let your young adult make a certain decision. What wisdom can you share with other parents facing a similar situation?
- Share an experience you and family members had when discernment was ongoing, taking several twists and turns, until you and your family arrived at a final decision.
- How do you understand the difference between the decision you arrive at in discernment and your faithfulness to the *process* of discernment? Consider times when you could see the difference.

CHAPTER 15: DISCERNMENT AND FAMILY WELL-BEING

- Family spirituality and family well-being go hand in hand. Does this statement ring true to your experience?
- Describe the home you've always dreamed of. What is getting in the way of fulfilling this dream?
- How would you respond to a spouse who prefers a more directive approach to parenting?
- In your family, how might discernment foster reconciliation?